DRIBBLES

Tosi Productions, LLC
Goffstown, New Hampshire

copyright © 2007 Thomas & Heidi Tosi

"Dribbles" motion picture screenplay copyright © 2003 Thomas Tosi

No part of this book may be reproduced in any form by electronic or mechanical means, including information storage and retrieval systems, without permission in writing from the publisher, except by a reviewer, who may quote brief passages in a review. Educators wishing to reproduce part or all of this work should contact Tosi Productions, LLC.

ISBN 978-0-6151-4509-9

Printed in the United States of America
First Edition 2007

Tosi Productions, LLC
PO Box 406
Goffstown, NH 03045
www.tosiproductions.com
www.dribblesmovie.com

Contents

Dribbles   1
an original screenplay by Thomas Tosi

Production Guide   123

Motion Picture End Credits   133

DRIBBLES

an original screenplay
by Thomas Tosi

BLACK.

A RUMBLING ECHO builds.

It is a sound like distant THUNDER approaching.

The THUNDER passes... then returns.

Rhythmically.

Passes... then returns.

FADE IN:

INT. LAKESHORE HIGH SCHOOL GYM, COURT - NIGHT

A crudely painted mural of a knight on horseback, jousting.

The SOUND OF THUNDER approaches again.

The knight shudders as if the painted horse were galloping across the field of honor.

As we pull away from the mural, we see the knight is surrounded by other roughly painted figures – teenage athletes.

We pull even further away to see that the mural is painted on a gymnasium wall. FORTY, SWEATING, TEENAGE BOYS are running suicide drills, creating the THUNDER. They stampede toward the camera. Reaching a painted line on the gymnasium floor, they stop and reverse direction like a herd of migratory animals driven by instinct.

The CREDITS are SUPERIMPOSED over a MONTAGE of basketball tryouts.

The three-man-weave.

Stomp drills.

Chest passes.

Re-bound drills.

The MONTAGE focuses in on one kid in particular, DAVID MCNEIL. David is of average height and build. He doesn't have the body of an athlete, but he's not out of shape either. There's a determination and intensity about him. Still, he doesn't fit in with the crowd. He's wearing cargo shorts, battered skateboarding sneakers and colored socks.

Out of sync in all the drills, he's obviously never played organized sports, but he's putting everything he's got into it. DAN STEPHAN, the boys' basketball coach, and CARL JOINER, his assistant, supervise the workout and make notes of what they see.

The MONTAGE ends with Stephan BLOWING a WHISTLE.

> STEPHAN
> Alright, gentlemen, let's finish up.
> Twenty laps then hit the showers.

With the bleachers retracted into the walls, the gym is the width of three basketball courts, so twenty laps after a strenuous tryout will be next to impossible.

The one kid who still looks alive, EDDIE COLES, runs off and begins.

The rest of the boys, hair matted down onto foreheads, shirts soaked with sweat and breath coming hard, obediently trot off and follow.

Joiner gives Stephan a questioning glance as if to ask if twenty laps isn't a bit too much.

> STEPHAN (CONT'D)
> If I drive 'em hard enough, I won't need
> to make any cuts – they'll make 'em for
> me.

The out-of-step kid, David, breaks off from the pack and runs past Stephan and Joiner. Running by the athletic office, going down the entrance to the locker rooms, David looks ill.

> JOINER
> There goes one.

One of the gym doors opens almost hitting Eddie and some of the other running boys. A tall, alarmingly skinny old man enters. He wears a Lancers wool cap and the baggy trousers of his custodian's uniform have dried urine stains in the crotch.

                    EDDIE
            Watch it, retard.

DRIBBLES, the man who has entered, is carrying an ancient VHS camera. He's startled by the boys stampeding by him and he edges along the wall, as if afraid he will be run down. When he sees a wide opening, he steps out into the clear and walks over to the coach and his assistant.

                   DRIBBLES
               (holding up his camera
                and imitating a trumpet
                      charge)
            Dah-dah-dah-dum da-DAHHH!

Joiner looks away, embarrassed, not wanting to deal with Dribbles. Like many people, he's put off by the old man's slovenly appearance and eccentric behavior. Stephan, however, looks genuinely glad to see him.

                   STEPHAN
            Hey, hey! Dribbles Lucas-Berg! Little
            early for game films isn't it? These are
            just tryouts, buddy.

                   DRIBBLES
            Not too early! Never too early to learn
            from mistakes!

Dribbles walks past Joiner.

                   DRIBBLES (CONT'D)
            Well, gotta take a piss.

Joiner watches disgusted as Dribbles walks off toward the boys' locker room.

> JOINER
> I thought he died or something.

> STEPHAN
> Thought? Or hoped?

> JOINER
> I got nothing against him. It's just embarrassing having a feeb mascot.

> STEPHAN
> Well, as long as you don't have anything against him...

David emerges from the locker room, spits into a garbage barrel and runs off to rejoin the others, running even harder than before.

Even though Eddie is tiring, he's still running faster than any of the other boys. He catches up with David and paces him.

> EDDIE
> (looking back toward the locker room where Dribbles has gone)
> I see our mascot's back this year.

David is too winded to reply. The running is causing him pain. Eddie looks down at David's colored socks.

> EDDIE (CONT'D)
> Nice socks.

Eddie turns up the steam and blows past David.

Dribbles' YELLING VOICE can be heard echoing out of the boys' locker room.

> DRIBBLES (O.S.)
> Pukey! Pukey! Pukey!

Joiner gives the coach a contemptuous look as if to say "I told you so."

Dribbles comes out of the locker room, still yelling at the top of his lungs.

> DRIBBLES (CONT'D)
> Barforama! Technicolor Yawn! Ralph!
> Ralphy Boy! To the Mooooon, Norton!
> Get the ol' sawdust.

Some of the boys break out in laughter and stop running. The rest of the boys just stop running, grateful for the disruption.

> STEPHAN
> (to Joiner)
> I think he's trying to say that someone has vomited in the boys' room.
> (to the boys)
> O.K., that's it for tonight.

INT. BOYS' LOCKER ROOM, LAKESHORE HIGH - NIGHT

THREE BOYS head in toward the lockers and as they pass a row of sinks, they see that someone has vomited in one of them.

> BOY #1
> Sweet!

> BOY #2
> God, now I feel sick.

> BOY #3
> Oooh, tasty.

The coach and Joiner enter with some of the other boys and look at the sink. The coach looks around and finds a SMALL KID heading for the lockers.

> STEPHAN
> Hey kid, you want to make this team?

Even exhausted, the kid brightens.

> KID
> Yes sir!

                    STEPHAN
            Clean out that sink, O.K.

INT. LAKESHORE HIGH GYM - NIGHT

Stephan and Joiner come out of the locker room, just as the last few stragglers walk toward the door. David is in this last group. The coach pulls him aside while the others enter.

                    STEPHAN
            You get sick in there from running laps?

David answers in a defiant tone. Like the basketball drills, it doesn't suit him – it's not his natural state.

                    DAVID
            Sorry.

                    STEPHAN
            Why'd you come back out?

                    DAVID
            I wanna be on this team.

                    STEPHAN
            Sophomore?

                    DAVID
            Junior.

                    STEPHAN
            Never went out for the team before.

David shakes his head no.

                    STEPHAN (CONT'D)
            You're in my class. What's your name?

                    DAVID
            David McNeil.

                    STEPHAN
            You get sick like that again, McNeil, you
            stop. It's not good for you.

                    DAVID
          I wanna...

                    STEPHAN
          I know.

He waves David off. David heads for the locker room, but Stephan calls him back.

                    STEPHAN (CONT'D)
          McNeil. Nothing personal, but
          sometimes wanting it isn't enough, O.K.?
          We'll see.

INT. LAKESHORE HIGH LOCKER ROOM - NIGHT

David sits on a wooden bench, undressing. The room is steamy from the showers. Most of the other boys have finished taking theirs already and are getting dressed.

All around the sounds can be heard of the SHOWERS, LOCKER DOORS SLAMMING, boys SINGING, SHOUTING, LAUGHING, and CURSING.

A boy with average looks and an athletic build comes walking over to David. The boy, CHRISTIAN JONES, is soaking wet. He wraps a towel around his waist as he approaches David.

David is pulling off his colored socks. Painful blisters have erupted on his soles. The dye from the socks has turned his feet blue.

                    CHRISTIAN
          Looks like you've been in Italy stompin'
          grapes.

David looks up at him. His mind was elsewhere, he didn't get it.

                    CHRISTIAN (CONT'D)
          Only kidding. It's just kind of weird
          seeing you here.

Eddie walks by and snaps his towel off of Christian's calf. There is a
LOUD POP and Christian jumps. Eddie laughs.

                    DAVID
          Wow, they really do that here? I thought
          that was just in underarm commercials.

Eddie momentarily debates beating the crap out of David, decides he's not
worth it, then walks off.

                    CHRISTIAN
          You don't want to get him pissed off at
          you.
                    (inspecting his calf)
          Look what he did to me – and I'm his
          FRIEND.

                    DAVID
          Why?

INT. CHRISTIAN'S CAR, NEIGHBORHOOD - NIGHT

David is silent, as Christian drives slowly, looking at the houses. They are in a blue-collar neighborhood of the small city of Lakeshore. It is the fall and a scattering of leaves blows down the sidewalks.

> CHRISTIAN
> You'll haveta tell me which one again. I don't think I can find your new house in the dark.

David does not respond. He's sullen. Christian can sense the tension and he tries to break it.

> CHRISTIAN (CONT'D)
> Man, I ache all over.
> (pause)
> I envy you.

> DAVID
> What? And you don't think I'm sore?

> CHRISTIAN
> Yeah, but for you there's only one tryout left before cuts, I've got to go through this all season.

Christian laughs but David falls silent.

> CHRISTIAN (CONT'D)
> Hey, I'm just kidding. You've been acting weird ever since your father...
> (pause)
> C'mon, you don't really expect to make the team anyway, do you?

> DAVID
> I'll make this team.

> CHRISTIAN
> Why? You never gave a crap about sports before.

> DAVID
> Stop here.

                        CHRISTIAN
                This is it?

David turns and leans into the back seat of Christian's car and comes up with his duffel bag and a basketball.

                        DAVID
                Can I borrow this?

                        CHRISTIAN
                Sure...
                        (taking a look outside)
                Hey, this isn't your house.

David scrambles out of the car. Christian turns the lights and ignition off and follows.

EXT. DAVID'S NEIGHBORHOOD - NIGHT

David runs off into the dark. Christian follows.

                        CHRISTIAN
                Wait up! Where are you going?

EXT. PLAYGROUND - NIGHT

A street light illuminates one end of an asphalt basketball court. David comes running up, drops his bag at the edge of the court, dribbles out and begins shooting.

Christian comes running into the light, walks out onto the court and stops.

                        CHRISTIAN
                Haven't you had enough of this for one
                night?

David doesn't reply. He's dead serious and just keeps shooting hoops. He's getting a fair percentage of his shots in, but he stands flat footed when he shoots.

Christian walks absently over to the side of the court. He picks up a handful of small rocks and throws them, one at a time, at the metal backboard making it RING OUT.

> CHRISTIAN (CONT'D)
> You got a hell of a set-shot there, kid.
> It'll come in handy – if you ever play a
> team of pygmies.

Christian grabs a rebound, dribbles out away from the hoop, stops, turns, and executes a beautiful jump shot. The ball arcs gracefully in the glare of the street light, then swishes through the hoop. Nothing but net.

> CHRISTIAN (CONT'D)
> You ought to try this new thing they
> invented. It's called the jump shot.

David makes no response to this, instead just grabs a rebound and continues shooting. He makes fewer of his shots than before. Christian begins guarding David, one-on-one. David goes to shoot. It's another set shot. Christian easily slaps the ball away.

David is flustered, but doggedly goes after the rebound and continues the one-on-one. Christian blocks David again and the ball swipes the side of David's face, scuffing his cheek.

Christian grabs the loose ball, puts it in the hoop and stops, assuming they are finished. David picks up the ball, however, and continues playing.

Christian momentarily stares at his friend in disbelief.

> CHRISTIAN (CONT'D)
> I thought you were into painting and
> stuff. What is it you suddenly have to
> prove?

Alone on the court, in the small circle of light, David continues.

DISSOLVE TO:

INT. MCNEIL HOUSE, DAVID'S ROOM - DAY

We're CLOSE on David's face while he sleeps and even in sleep there is tension. A BUZZER can be heard, though it is not yet clear where this sound is coming from – could be a gymnasium scoreboard.

As we complete the dissolve into the room and the camera maneuvers, it becomes apparent that the sound is David's alarm clock sitting on dresser near the bed.

David flings his pillow at the clock and knocks it over into an open sock drawer.

Though muffled, the clock continues BUZZING. We work in CLOSE and see amid the socks and junk in the drawer is a deliberately torn photograph.

It's a TEAM PHOTO OF BASKETBALL PLAYERS circa the mid-eighties. The team members wear championship jackets. We focus on one player who bears a strong resemblance to David.

INT. DAN STEPHAN'S CLASSROOM - DAY

It is Lakeshore High's policy that all coaches also be teachers. Dan Stephan teaches Civics.

There are approximately twenty students in Stephan's class. Recognizable faces are David and Eddie. The class members sit in groups, four to a table.

At Eddie's table is a thin, greasy, SKATER-TYPE BOY. Their mutual disgust of one another is obvious from their body language.

>   STEPHAN
>   ...alright then, put the Patriot Act into a
>   context that you can relate to. Lockers.
>   The school can search them. Doesn't
>   need a reason – that O.K.?

A GIRL near the front of the room answers without raising her hand. She's rather scantily clad for a school setting.

>   CIVICS GIRL
>   Doesn't matter, if you complain about
>   something like that, they automatically
>   think you're doing something wrong.

>   STEPHAN
>   Are you?

                    CIVICS GIRL
          Go ahead and search my locker. I'm not
          hiding anything.

                    STEPHAN
               (with a quick scan of her
                minimalist clothing)
          Which doesn't mean you shouldn't
          occasionally cover up.

A SOFT RIPPLE OF LAUGHTER from those in the class who got it.

There is a KNOCK AT THE DOOR. A girl, MARY TODD, enters and approaches Stephan. She hands him a note.

                    STEPHAN (CONT'D)
          O.K., welcome to our class. We'll take
          care of introductions later.
               (he motions her to sit)
          Columbine.

That's an attention getter.

We focus on Mary while she makes her way through the room. There are empty seats at several tables, including David's.

                    STEPHAN (CONT'D)
          An individual's right to privacy or the
          right of all of us to be in a safe
          environment. What do you think?

Though not stunning, Mary is pretty and, more importantly, new – so, of course, all the boys check her out as she moves back through the room.

David is the exception. He is intent upon a notebook, hidden from view behind a stack of text books on his table. He pays no attention to Mary. For this reason, she heads in his direction.

Mary takes the seat but David's textbooks are stacked on the table in front of her. He doesn't move them. He's too intent on whatever he's working on.

                    STEPHAN (O.S.) (CONT'D)
               C'mon. How far can and should a
               government go?

Mary finally slides the books aside herself and when she does so, she sees
David had been drawing a page full of QUICK SKETCHES OF
VARIOUS MEMBERS OF THE CLASS.

David shoots her a look.

                         MARY
                    (moving the books back
                    into position)
               Sorry.

                         DAVID
               It's O.K.

                         SKATER-KID
               They're gonna go as far as they can –
               governments suck.

A round of GIGGLES AND LAUGHTER.

                         STEPHAN
               Governments... suck.

More GIGGLES. Eddie is irritated. Stephan sees this.

> STEPHAN (CONT'D)
> Well, there's an opinion. You can say
> that. 'Course, I wouldn't if I were you. A
> government's the only thing keeping guys
> like him...
> > (indicates Eddie)
> ...from beating the crap out of guys like
> you.

What was meant as a social commentary is taken as a compliment by Eddie and much of the rest of the class.

INT. PIC N' SAVE SUPERMARKET, FROZEN FOODS - NIGHT

David is grocery shopping with his mother and AUNT ANNIE. David's mother, SARAH, is just thirty-five, having had David when she was just out of high school.

Perhaps it is because of this small age difference that Sarah is not the authority figure she should be.

Aunt Annie is Sarah's little sister. She's just thirty and even less of an authority figure.

Annie works at an antique clothing store called "Seams Like Old Times" and she enjoys making a fashion statement – loudly.

David looks disgusted as Annie fills up the shopping cart with low carb frozen dinners. She tosses in the frozen dinners in groups of three.

                    ANNIE
              (as each trio of dinners
                lands in the cart)
          Monday – Tuesday – Wednesday –
          Thursday...

INT. PIC N' SAVE SUPERMARKET, CHECK-OUT - NIGHT

Annie leads the carriage into a check-out lane. She immediately pulls a celebrity entertainment newspaper off the rack and rifles through it.

                    ANNIE
          You know, I really think Gollum was on
          low carb. Seriously, think about it. You
          can count the guy's ribs, he only eats fish
          and meat, he spits out the Elvish bread,
          and doesn't like the sound of 'taters.

Sarah LAUGHS but nothing seems to amuse David.

He looks down toward the register, sees the customer in front of them and he quickly turns away, embarrassed. The person in front of them in line is Dribbles.

David does not want to be recognized.

Dribbles is arguing with the girl behind the check-out. David cannot help glancing over to see what's happening.

The argument is over money. Among his groceries, Dribbles has five boxes of cake mix.

Dribbles' eccentricities are in full bloom. The CHECK-OUT GIRL is trying to be polite but her patience is wearing thin.

                    CHECK-OUT GIRL
          ...put something back, you're six dollars
          and forty nine cents short.

> DRIBBLES
> I'm good for it, I'm good for it! Everyone
> knows me. Honest man is what I am!
> (turns to Annie, David
> and Sarah)
> Ask 'em, go ahead.

David turns away again.

> CHECK-OUT GIRL
> Sir, I'm sorry, but we don't offer credit.

> DRIBBLES
> I don't want no whoopie-doopin' charity!

> CHECK-OUT GIRL
> I said credit, not charity.

> DRIBBLES
> Well that's different, I'll take credit.

The shift manager comes over to see what the commotion is all about. Sarah digs in her purse and comes out with seven dollars. She hands it to David.

> SARAH
> (hushed voice)
> Go on and give this to him.
> (indicates Dribbles)

                    DAVID
          No!

David shoves the money back at her. Sarah is surprised and angry.

                    MANAGER
          Hi ya, Dribbles.

                    CHECK-OUT GIRL
          We don't offer credit.

                    MANAGER
          It's O.K., Shannon. How short is he?

                    CHECK-OUT GIRL
          Six forty-nine.

                    MANAGER
          You're all set Dribbles, get it to us when
          you can.

Dribbles has been vindicated. He gathers his groceries to leave.

                    DRIBBLES
          I told ya, they all know me.

EXT. DAVID'S HOUSE - MORNING

It is a bright, crisp morning. There are pockets of activity in the neighborhood as people leave for work and school.

White plumes of exhaust billow behind cars and frost stencils windows in spite of the fact that the brightly colored leaves just began to fall a week ago. Sarah is scraping the windshield of her beat-up old '84 Caprice wagon. Annie backs a three-year-old Suburu out of the driveway and stops near her.

                    SARAH
          You're up and about early.

                    ANNIE
          Opening for Deena.

David comes out of the house wearing jeans and a T-shirt.

                    SARAH
               Put a jacket on.

David ducks back inside the house, slamming the door.

                    SARAH (CONT'D)
               He's so angry lately. Used to be such a
               sensitive kid.
                         (pause)
               I wonder if I did the right thing.

                    ANNIE
               I think you did.

                    SARAH
               I thought so too. I know I did for Alex
               and me. I'm not so sure about David
               anymore, though.

Annie puts her car in drive.

                    ANNIE
               Chin up kid, it'll be fine.

She drives off.

A kid about David's age comes down the sidewalk, riding a bicycle. The BIKE KID is bundled up with a jacket, fingerless gloves and a wool cap.

We see his puffs of breath and his red cheeks as he rides along with one hand on the handlebar and the other carrying a graffiti covered spiral binder. As he passes Sarah...

                    SARAH
                    (indicating frost)
               Do you believe this? Already?

The kid smiles, nods and keeps riding. David re-emerges from the house, this time wearing a jacket. He walks over to the car, goes around to the passenger side and hops in, leaving his mother to finish scraping.

She clears the glass in front of him. There's tension between them.

EXT. LAKESHORE HIGH - DAY

Clusters of kids converge on the school.

A BELL RINGS.

INT. LAKESHORE HIGH, HALLWAY - DAY

A mass of confusion fills the hallway, TALKING VOICES, YELLING, LAUGHTER, and SLAMMING LOCKER DOORS. Paper Halloween decorations are taped to some of the classroom doors.

David makes his way through the crowd. He looks over to a foyer and is stopped by something. A cafeteria table is set-up. A COUPLE OF WOMEN, most likely students' mothers, are setting a spread of baked goods on the table.

A hand made sign behind them reads, "Lancers Boosters Club - Bake Sale."

What's stopped David is the sight of Dribbles, in his custodian's uniform, helping to load up the table – with boxes of homemade cupcakes.

Suddenly, a CRASHING SOUND is heard. David wheels around. Eddie has thrown the Skater-kid from Civics up against the lockers and is beating him severely.

Eddie's tight muscles pump as he pounds away at the kid. Dribbles runs in to break things up but Eddie throws an elbow back which catches Dribbles in the chest and knocks him to the floor.

A crowd of students, unaware of who started the fight or even what it's about, automatically cheer on Eddie, the popular athlete.

A MALE TEACHER runs in and breaks things up but he's late and sees only the end of the scuffle.

> TEACHER
> Alright! Knock it off! Knock it off!

Eddie shifts his wild gaze from the kid to the teacher. The teacher involuntarily backs up a step, afraid. Dribbles has crawled off into the crowd. The fire in Eddie's eyes dims a little. The teacher calms down.

> TEACHER (CONT'D)
> (to the crowd)
> You people have someplace to be now.

A girl near Eddie, SHERI, is almost in tears. Eddie puts his arm around her and they walk off. The crowd parts in front of them as though they are royalty.

> TEACHER (CONT'D)
> I don't get paid for this.

A CLOSE-UP of David shows that he was fascinated by this exchange.

David reacts as he suddenly feels his pants being tugged downward. He looks down to see that Dribbles is standing up by grabbing a locker handle with one hand and David's cargos with the other. A RIPPLE OF LAUGHTER erupts from some NEARBY STUDENTS.

Quickly adjusting his pants, David violently tugs free from Dribbles and the old man falls hard to the floor again.

> DRIBBLES
> Oopsie.

Dribbles extends his hand to David for help. David looks from the laughing students to Dribbles and turns away.

On the SOUNDTRACK, the DISTANT THUNDER rises... then falls... rises and falls.

DISSOLVE TO:

INT. LAKESHORE HIGH, GYM - NIGHT

A MONTAGE of basketball tryouts similar to the opening sequence...

Lay-up drills...

Foul shooting...

Scrimmaging...

David has improved noticeably since the first tryout and he's knocking himself out again but he's still not one of the better players. He's not quite worked his way up to average. It's no longer incomprehensible that he might make the team, just unlikely.

Stephan and Joiner pay scrupulous attention to everything that goes on, keeping notes.

Throughout the MONTAGE, Stephan can be heard in VOICE-OVER calling off a roll.

>STEPHAN (V.O.)
>...Cole – Dwight – Finn – Fennwick – Jones – Kensington – Martel – Michaud – Railsbeck – Russo...

The MONTAGE ends and Stephan is standing in front of the group of boys. Tryouts are obviously over as the boys have showered, gathered their belongings and are sitting on the court. As Stephan reads the names off of the list, the boys who hear their names are informally congratulated.

>STEPHAN (CONT'D)
>Tenney and Washington. That's fifteen, that's all the slots I have, congratulations.

A fair number of those who didn't make the team have already started walking off the court. David is standing near the team members.

> STEPHAN (CONT'D)
> I know what this sounds like, but I really did have to make some tough decisions. You underclassmen who got cut, I expect to see you out here next year. The rest of you be here tomorrow night. Thank you gentlemen.

Stephan heads off toward the athletic office near the locker rooms. Some of the boys on the court, including Eddie and Christian, let out celebration whoops and slap each other five. They head toward the doors.

David, alone, still sits in the middle of the court. Christian, heading off with the others, turns and sees him. He comes back over.

> CHRISTIAN
> You know these tryouts are a big show. Most of these guys been playing together on travel teams since they were eight.

There is no response from David who merely stares over near the exit where Eddie is pulling on his state championship varsity jacket.

> CHRISTIAN (CONT'D)
> Hey, what were you thinkin' anyway? College scholarship? Shot at the NBA? C'mon.

> DAVID
> I'm not stupid, Christian, I just...

> CHRISTIAN
> What?

David nods toward Eddie.

> DAVID
> I just wanted a jacket.

Christian looks over toward Eddie, but it still takes a moment to sink in. When it does, Christian cannot stifle the laugh.

> CHRISTIAN
> You just wanted a state championship jacket. That's all. No big deal. But you're not stupid...

> DAVID
> Screw you.

> CHRISTIAN
> I don't know what's happened to you, man, I really don't.

Christian leaves him. After a moment, David also heads for the exit.

As he passes the athletic office, David sees Stephan talking to Eddie.

INT. LAKESHORE HIGH, ATHLETIC OFFICE - NIGHT

> STEPHAN
> ...lot of expectations this year, Mr. Coles. You're going to be all right with some pressure?

Eddie's no longer the animal from the hallway, but a clean-cut American hero.

> EDDIE
> Yes sir.

EXT. LAKESHORE HIGH GYM - NIGHT

Some of the boys from tryouts are being picked-up by their parents and some are bundling up for the ride home on bicycles but most have driven themselves here. Those who made the team are hanging around talking and joking. The others leave quickly and quietly as though they have not only been cut from the team, but from this entire social set.

Christian and Eddie are leaning on Christian's car, talking. They seem suddenly more serious than the others.

> CHRISTIAN
> Do either your parents know?

Eddie shakes his head no.

> CHRISTIAN (CONT'D)
> Well, what does Sheri wanna do?

> EDDIE
> Sheri's... I don't know, Sheri's crazy, man.

> CHRISTIAN
> She wants to keep it?

Christian sees David walking off in the distance.

> EDDIE
> No, I do.

This was unexpected and Christian shoots a glance at Eddie. Eddie's upset. Before he tears up, he turns away.

EDDIE (CONT'D)
                  (walking off)
               You tell anyone... friend or not, I'll bust
               you wide open.

Christian looks after him a moment, then off toward David.

                    CHRISTIAN
               Hey, David. C'mon, I'll give you a ride.

David is far away now and just keeps walking.

                    CHRISTIAN (CONT'D)
                  (to himself)
               Be like that.

EXT. LAKESHORE, DAVID'S NEIGHBORHOOD - NIGHT

David slowly walks home, shivering against the chill air. Up and off to his left is a highway overpass that crosses over a lake inlet. Traffic RUMBLES from the highway. A tractor trailer truck BLARES ITS HORN, stopping David. He turns and looks toward the overpass. The truck THUNDERS on into the night.

EXT. LAKESHORE, HIGHWAY OVERPASS - NIGHT

David scrambles up an embankment, over the guardrail and up onto the overpass. He looks small on the concrete, in the glare of the highway lamps. Cars and trucks blow past him, their turbulence ripping at his jacket.

David runs part way down the overpass, turns and begins to back-pedal. He is to the point where the overpass crosses over the lake inlet. He faces the traffic and sticks his thumb out.

Several cars pass, then a tractor-trailer downshifts and slows. Its AIR BRAKES HUFF and WHEEZE as it pulls over twenty yards ahead of him. David runs to it.

His run becomes a trot... then a walk. When he gets to the passenger door, he opens it, but does not climb in. The DRIVER looks at him curiously.

                    DAVID
                  (apologetically)
               Go ahead... sorry.

                              DRIVER
                         Suit yourself, kid.

David closes the door and the truck pulls away from him. He turns to look at the side of the road. He is over the lake inlet. He walks to the guardrail.

David tosses his gym bag into the lake.

EXT. LAKESHORE HIGH - DAY

The parking lot is full, school is in session.

INT. LAKESHORE HIGH, HALLWAY - DAY

In between classes, the halls are mobbed. Coach Stephan makes his way through the throng. He pulls a notice out of his clipboard and tapes it to the wall.

CLOSE-UP NOTICE

"Don't BECOME a statistic – KEEP them! The Boy's Varsity Basketball Squad Needs a Manager! Fun! Excitement! Travel! See Coach Stephan, Rm. 319."

INT. DAN STEPHAN'S CLASSROOM - DAY

Students are shuffling into the class and taking their seats. Stephan has not yet arrived, he must be out hanging up the last few notices.

David plops his books down on his table and takes off his jacket. Mary is already in her seat beside him. She looks up at him and smiles.

                              MARY
                 Hi.

                              DAVID
                            (absently)
                 Hi.

Putting his jacket on the back of his seat, David notices that on the back of Mary's seat is an athletic jacket from another school. The embroidery on the jacket's sleeve proclaims, "State Champs 2003 Field Hockey." Stitched in below that is "Mary – Manager."

David stares at the jacket. Mary catches him and wonders what the heck he's looking at.

> MARY
> (explaining)
> From my old school...

> DAVID
> You get a jacket for being team manager?

> MARY
> Sure, manager's part of the team.
> (pause)
> Thinking of going out for field hockey?

David's mind is elsewhere, he doesn't reply. Mary looks at him a moment, pumps up her courage a notch and then...

> MARY (CONT'D)
> You like movies?

David's caught off guard. He stares at her dumbly.

EXT. STREETS OF LAKESHORE - NIGHT

Sarah's Caprice wagon rattles down the street. It is just entering Lakeshore's business district.

Groups of costumed kids, most with their parents, make their way up and down the sidewalks – trick-or-treating.

INT. CAPRICE - NIGHT

While David drives and Mary sits on the passenger side, it's obvious from their body language that they're both a little nervous.

> MARY
> I've never been out with a jock before.

> DAVID
> I'm not a jock.

MARY
I asked a girl in class about you and she said you were going out for the basketball team...

DAVID
I did, but it's the first time I've ever gone out for a sport before.

MARY
Oh, so that explains it.

DAVID
Explains what?

MARY
Nothing.

DAVID
You started this. What?

MARY
Well, she was kind of laughing when she said it.

EXT. STREETS OF LAKESHORE - NIGHT

The Caprice approaches an intersection showing a green light.

Someone wearing a white sheet with eye holes darts out from a side street, awkwardly riding a bicycle. They shoot out right in front of the car.

INT. CAPRICE - NIGHT

David slams on the brakes.

DAVID
Hold on!

The Caprice skids to a halt, narrowly missing the person on the bike. Mary is thrown up then back in her seat.

EXT. STREETS OF LAKESHORE - NIGHT

The front tires of the Caprice catch the person's ghost sheet and pull him off balance. He struggles out from under the sheet and rides away. The man on the bike is not fazed by this close encounter. He turns and waves pleasantly. When he does, we see that he is Dribbles.

INT. CAPRICE - NIGHT

>   MARY
>   He didn't even look!
>
>   DAVID
>   Dribbles.
>
>   MARY
>   Is he crazy?

When David speaks to Mary, he is no longer the angry young man. She brings out the thoughtful person he used to be.

>   DAVID
>   Yeah, he kind of is.

The engine has stalled. David re-starts it and pulls away.

EXT. EMPIRE THEATER - NIGHT

The Empire Theater used to be a grand old movie palace. It now gets by as a revival house for classic movies.

Its marquee tonight reads: "HALLOWEEN SPECIAL, THE THING."

A line of people, some of them in costume, stretches around the block. As the Caprice coasts down the street, a MAN comes out of the THEATER and begins speaking to the crowd...

>   THEATER MAN
>   ...singles only, we just have a few single
>   seats left for the seven-fifteen show...

A few people step forward and enter the THEATER. Most of the crowd, disappointed, disperses.

INT. CAPRICE - NIGHT

David and Mary cruise by slowly, watching the crowd leave.

> MARY
> There's the second showing...?

> DAVID
> Yeah, but what're we going to do for two hours?

INT. THE CORNER DRUG STORE - NIGHT

In addition to its health care products, The Corner Drug Store stocks a selection of Halloween candy, makeup, and rubber masks. Most of the good masks are gone. David and Mary are kneeling in the aisle sorting through, and trying on, what's left.

Mary puts on a flamboyant, hot pink, eye mask – embellished with sequins and feathers. David pulls a rubber mask over his head – he's an angry clown.

> DAVID
> This is so... stupid.

> MARY
> Oh, it's you!

They both laugh.

EXT. LAKESHORE NEIGHBORHOOD - NIGHT

David and Mary walk along, leaving the Caprice parked at the side of the road. In addition to her mask, Mary also has a cape and a wand. To make room for her cape, she has her field hockey jacket tied around her waist.

They stop behind a tree and watch THREE TINY TRICK-OR-TREATERS head for a house.

> MARY
> (cooing)
> Oh, look! Look!

Mary looks down at the paper bag in which their masks came, and then up at the house again.

                    DAVID
          You wouldn't...

Leaving David at the sidewalk, Mary goes up to the house and trick-or-treats.

                    DAVID (CONT'D)
          I don't believe it.

She gets something.

                    DAVID (CONT'D)
          She got something.

Mary trots back and they go off down the sidewalk, laughing.

EXT. TREE-LINED STREET - NIGHT

Mary pulls two mini-candy bars from her paper bag. She offers one to the angry clown.

                    MARY
          Sweet?

The angry clown takes the candy bar, stops, and stares at her.

                    MARY (CONT'D)
          What?

David pulls off the mask.

                    DAVID
          I bet you're one of those kids who can
          always think of something fun to do on
          rainy days.

Mary is getting chilly. She takes her cape off and puts on her jacket.

                    MARY
          There's no trick to being fun, just don't let
          what other people might think of you
          stop you from doing what you want.

                    DAVID
          Immune from peer pressure?

                    MARY
          Sure.

                    DAVID
          Why'd you manage the field hockey team
          and get that jacket?

                    MARY
          I don't care about the jacket. I managed
          the team 'cause it was a good time with
          my friends.

                    DAVID
          Yeah, but that jacket's kind of a trophy.
          It must mean something to you.

                    MARY
          Means I won't get cold.

INT. MCNEIL HOUSE, LIVING ROOM - NIGHT

Sarah is sitting Indian style on the couch. She is surrounded by paperwork and has a check book register open in front of her. She sips at a cup of coffee and does computations on a calculator.

Headlights from outside shine in through the window and sweep across the room. The CAPRICE can be heard PULLING INTO THE DRIVEWAY. A CAR DOOR OPENS AND CLOSES.

David enters. He is surprised to see that his mother is still awake. When he speaks, David is the angry young man again.

                    DAVID
          Worried about your car?

> SARAH
> Doing the budget.

> DAVID
> Kind of late for that, isn't it?

> SARAH
> Your father isn't exactly an accountant.
> He left the checkbook in a bit of a mess...

> DAVID
> (leaving the room)
> I guess leaving things in a mess was his specialty.

> SARAH
> David...

INT. MCNEIL HOUSE, DAVID'S ROOM - NIGHT

David enters the room and throws the angry clown mask on the floor. Sitting on the edge of the bed, he pulls the candy bar Mary gave him out of his pocket.

He relaxes, takes a bite of the sweet, and thinks of her.

INT. HALLWAY, LAKESHORE HIGH – DAY

David rips Coach Stephan's notice about basketball manager off of the wall.

INT. LAKESHORE HIGH HALLWAY, OUTSIDE STEPHAN'S CLASS – DAY

Looking into the classroom from the window on the door, we can see David talking with Coach Stephan. They shake hands. Students on their way to and from classes pass up and down. Christian is opening a locker almost directly across from Stephan's classroom. David makes his way out into the hall and over to Christian.

                    DAVID
            See you at practice tomorrow night.

Christian was not aware they were on speaking terms after their last meeting and he is not sure how to take this.

                    CHRISTIAN
            I don't think that's such a smart idea...

                    DAVID
            I'm part of the team.

Christian doesn't understand. Behind the two boys, Stephan is at the door to his classroom, talking to Dribbles who is leaning against his broom.

                    DAVID (CONT'D)
            I'm the new manager of the Lakeshore
            Lancers.

                    CHRISTIAN
            You're still after that stupid jacket...

                    STEPHAN
            McNeil!

David wheels around.

                    STEPHAN (CONT'D)
            You know Dribbles. You two will be
            working together.

                    DRIBBLES
            Pard-ner!

Students passing by in the hallway LAUGH and continue on their way. David is shocked.

                    CHRISTIAN
                    (smiles)
            Welcome to the team.

David turns back to look at Christian as an ear-piercing BUZZER SOUNDS. This sound carries over to...

INT. LAKESHORE HIGH GYM, COURT - NIGHT

The first game of the season is in progress. The FOUL BUZZER IS SOUNDING as a dorky player on the opposing team awkwardly tries to steal the ball from Eddie and fouls him.

Eddie puts up his free-throw and it swishes.

The near-capacity crowd roars.

At the end of the Lancer's bench, Dribbles dutifully films the action with his VHS camera. Beside him, David tries to make sense of the charts and graphs he has on his clipboard.

When watching the action, he cannot fill out the charts. When filling out the charts, he misses the action. One of the charts is merely an outline of a basketball court. The other is a list of the player names with columns labeled "FGA, FG, FTA, FT, TP, PF, TF, Steals, Assts." After Eddie's basket, David scribbles in a "1" beside Eddie's name under FGA.

Dribbles glances at the chart out of the corner of his eye...

                        DRIBBLES
      Wrongo!

David frantically erases the "1" and rewrites it under FG.

Christian steals the ball and takes it down the other end for a lay-up.

                      DRIBBLES (CONT'D)
      Wrong! Wrong! WRONG-O!

                      DAVID
      Hey shut up! I know what's going on.

The crowd is cheering after Christian's lay-up. David turns to the player beside him, Michaud.

                    DAVID (CONT'D)
          What happened?

                    MICHAUD
          Christian put in a lay-up.

                    DRIBBLES
          Jones, one F.G.!

David pulls out the chart with the outline of the basketball court.

                    DAVID
          Do you know what this is fo...?

He goes to show it to Michaud but...

                    STEPHAN
          Michaud!

Michaud jumps up and heads down to the coach. David holds the chart up so that the CHEERLEADERS behind the bench can see it.

                    DAVID
          I don't suppose any of you girls would
          know what...?

One of the girls SCREECHES. The basketball flies into David's hand, knocking the clipboard to the floor. The ball is followed almost immediately by a player from the opposing team who crashes into David's chair and knocks him over.

The player runs back out onto the court. David is sprawled out on the floor, looking up at seven cheerleaders.

The HEAD CHEERLEADER does not like the idea of David laying there, staring up at her.

> HEAD CHEERLEADER
> Go on back and play with your friend.
> (she indicates Dribbles)

Dribbles helps David back up and into his chair. David, embarrassed by the old man, tries to shake him off.

Undaunted, Dribbles picks up the charts and displays them for David.

> DRIBBLES
> When a guy shoots...

He writes a number on the court outline.

> DRIBBLES (CONT'D)
> When a guy makes it...
> (he circles the number)
> Ask me. I know lotsa stuff.

David rudely grabs the charts away from Dribbles.

Eddie puts in a shot from the field.

The crowd chants.

> CROWD
> ED-DIE! ED-DIE! ED-DIE!

A LITTLE BOY in the crowd holds up a piece of poster board with Eddie's number painted on it.

> DRIBBLES
> Coles, one field goal, assist, Jones.

When he's rifling off statistics, Dribbles is less eccentric. He's more focused and aware.

Reluctantly, David fills in the appropriate columns on the chart as per Dribbles' instructions.

Eddie puts in another shot from the field.

> DRIBBLES (CONT'D)
> Coles, field goal, assist, Russo.

David fills in the chart.

A REFEREE BLOWS a WHISTLE.

> DRIBBLES (CONT'D)
> Jones, second personal foul, team fouls, four.

David fills it in. Dribbles is beginning to irritate him. He glances over at the old man, then looks up and watches the action.

Christian puts in a field goal.

> DRIBBLES (CONT'D)
> Jones, field goal, no assist.

David has already filled it in.

> DAVID
> I got it. I got it.

The ball goes in the hoop.

David fills in the chart.

The REFEREE BLOWS his WHISTLE.

Dribbles still tapes and chants.

                        DRIBBLES
                Michaud, personal fouls, two, team fouls,
                five...

David fills in the chart.

Dribbles swish pans his camera to the far end of the court.

A player from the visiting team shoots.

The ball goes in the hoop.

Dribbles swish pans his camera up toward the scoreboard. A BUZZER SOUNDS. He's still rifling off statistics.

                        DRIBBLES (CONT'D)
                ...total points, Lakeshore sixty-five,
                Daleville...

CLOSE-UP Scoreboard "Home 65, Visitors 75 - Period 4, 00:00"

                        DRIBBLES (O.S.) (CONT'D)
                    (disappointment)
                ...seventy-five.

The crowd YELLS and BOO'S.

Dan Stephan looks up at the board, then leans over to the man working at the scorer's table, HARVE.

                        STEPHAN
                    (indicating board)
                Harve, turn the thing off buddy.

                        HARVE
                Won't do no good, Mr. Stephan, you
                buttered your bread...

                        STEPHAN
                    (looks to crowd)
                ...and they're gonna toast me.

Eddie storms angrily over to the bench and drop kicks a plastic water bottle up into the bleachers. The team heads toward the locker room.

                    STEPHAN (CONT'D)
                        (to Eddie)
                    Wrong sport.

Stephan turns to David.

                    STEPHAN (CONT'D)
                Get that bottle before some lucky fan
                takes home a souvenir.

David stands incredulous for a moment and then climbs under the bleachers. He makes his way through the jungle of crisscrossed steel supports. The floor under the bleachers is littered with paper cups, confetti and empty popcorn boxes.

The supports shudder as the crowd makes its way down to the exits.

                    MARY
                Hey there!

David looks up to see Mary peering down through the bleachers.

                    MARY (CONT'D)
                Watch'ya doin', trying to look up the girls'
                skirts?

David holds up the plastic water bottle.

                    DRIBBLES (O.S.)
                Thought you were the manager, not the
                whoopie-doopin' water boy.

David looks over to see Dribbles filming him through the steel supports. It makes him embarrassed and pissed off.

INT. LAKESHORE HIGH GYM, ATHLETIC OFFICE - NIGHT

Joiner is putting the practice basketballs back in the equipment closet. Stephan is sitting behind a desk, ripping pages out of a play book, crumpling them, and throwing them at a wastebasket. He misses every time.

David enters, hands his clipboards to Stephan and goes over to the sink to wash out the plastic bottle.

                        STEPHAN
                  (examining the charts)
            McNeil, these accurate?

                        DAVID
            Think so.

                        STEPHAN
            Damn.

A LOUD CRASH of METAL followed by SCREAMING startles them all.

                        FRANTIC WOMAN (O.S.)
            Someone get that animal off of my son!

Christian and some of the other players run by the door to the athletic office.

INT. LAKESHORE HIGH GYM - NIGHT

A metal door leading outside rumbles furiously. Christian, followed by the others, runs down to the door. When Christian pulls open the door, a bloody player from the other team falls backward into the gym. On top of him is Eddie. A FRANTIC WOMAN, the bloody boy's mother, is crying and tugging at Eddie.

Dribbles stands, taping the entire scene with his VHS camera.

INT. LAKESHORE HIGH TEAM ROOM - DAY

At first glance it appears as though we are just seeing Eddie's fight outside the gym from Dribbles' point of view.

But the image of the fight is very low resolution, poor contrast quality.

PULL BACK to reveal that we are in the team room and watching Dribbles' VHS footage of the fight. The footage is powerful – violent and bloody. The hand-held nature of the camera work adds to the intensity of the fight.

INT. LAKESHORE HIGH GYM, LOCKER ROOM - DAY

Christian, David, and two other team members are huddled near a locker that shares a wall with the team room.

>   CHRISTIAN
> They still watchin' the tape?

>   MICHAUD
>   (hushed voice)
> Shut up.

INT. LAKESHORE HIGH TEAM ROOM - DAY

On tape, Eddie is pummeling the player from the opposing team while the kid's mother tries to break it up. Christian and some of the other team members grab Eddie and pull him off the other boy.

A few static bars flicker across the screen and the image is replaced by electronic noise. The tape has ended. Joiner turns the lights on in the team room. Also in the room with him are Coach Stephan, Dribbles, and a middle-aged man we have not seen before, Lakeshore High principal WILLIAM BECKER.

>   PRINCIPAL BECKER
> I don't know, Dan. Maybe we can get
> away with suspending him for three
> games...

>   JOINER
>   (protesting)
> Coles is our best player.

Stephen shoots Joiner an angry look.

>   PRINCIPAL BECKER
> He's damn lucky they're not pressing
> charges.

Dribbles begins rewinding his tape.

                    STEPHAN
              (to Dribbles, honestly)
          Thank you.

                    JOINER
              (bitterly)
          Yeah, thanks a lot.

INT. LAKESHORE HIGH GYM, LOCKER ROOM - DAY

Michaud climbs out of the locker and quietly closes the door behind him.

                    MICHAUD
          Three game suspension.

                    DAVID
          That's it? You're kidding! They're still
          cleaning the blood out of the floor tiles
          out there!

                    CHRISTIAN
          You know what three games without our
          best player could do to this team? Or
          don't you want your precious jacket
          anymore? Besides, how do you know
          what happened? You don't know
          anything about Eddie.

INT. MCNEIL HOUSE, DAVID'S ROOM - DAY

David's bedroom is not the room of a jock. Assorted drawings and paintings are tacked to the walls. A bookshelf is full of hard-cover books and art supplies. David sits on the edge of his bed, putting on his sneakers. Beside him is an open window. The curtains blow inward. It's a crisp, late autumn day. David gets a draft from the open window and closes it. He slides open the drawer of the night table beside the bed and pulls out his wallet.

Beside the wallet, we notice once again the ripped photo of the ball players.

Walking down to the end of the bed, David picks up a brand new basketball, still in it's original package.

SARAH (O.S.)
David! Someone here for you!

INT. MCNEIL HOUSE, DOWNSTAIRS HALLWAY - DAY

David comes downstairs to find Sarah, Mary, and Aunt Annie. Sarah and Aunt Annie are halfway out the door. Mary is just standing politely waiting for him.

Annie is dressed in a wild outfit of black lace that's half goth and half Victoria's Secret.

SARAH
Here he is. You two have fun.

ANNIE
A basketball and a girl? David you're just absolutely full of surprises!

DAVID
(sarcastically)
Nice outfit.

ANNIE
Hey, some of us have to work for a living.

Sarah pulls Annie out the door with her.

EXT. PLAYGROUND, DAVID'S NEIGHBORHOOD - DAY

David and Mary are at the same basketball court where Christian threw a rock at the backboard. In the daytime, we see that the court is only part of a neighborhood playground.

A couple plays with their two young children in the sandbox. The trees are now bare and the only leaves that blow across the court are brown and withered. David dribbles and shoots his new ball.

Mary swings on a swing-set nearby. She's chilly and pulls the sleeves of her over-sized sweater down to cover her hands. It has the effect of making her seem vulnerable and quite adorable.

>   MARY
> What does your Aunt Annie do?

>   DAVID
> Huh?

>   MARY
> She said she was dressed for work?

>   DAVID
> Oh.
>   (laughing)
> She's not a prostitute, if that's what you were thinking...

That is what she was thinking.

>   MARY
> No.

>   DAVID
> She works in a clothing store called "Seams Like Old Times..." They sell second hand stuff – call it "Antique Clothing." SEAMS like old times. Get it?

Mary groans.

>   DAVID (CONT'D)
> Yeah, exactly.

>   MARY
> Your aunt lives with you guys?

David stops shooting hoops and walks over to the swing beside Mary and sits. He shakes his head no.

                    DAVID
          We live with her.

Mary looks confused.

                    DAVID (CONT'D)
          When my father walked out on my mom
          and me, she couldn't make the payments.

                    MARY
          Why'd he take off?

David is surprised. He starts swinging. Pumping vigorously, he works himself higher and higher.

                    DAVID
          Didn't you know? That's a question
          you're not supposed to ask.

                    MARY
          Sorry.

                    DAVID
          I'm kidding. I'm glad you asked. I hate it
          when people pretend like they're not
          interested.

He slows and stops swinging.

                    DAVID (CONT'D)
               Boredom I guess. Couldn't stick with it.
                         (laugh)
               That's the kicker!

Mary doesn't know what he's getting at.

                    DAVID (CONT'D)
               This guy who couldn't hold the same job
               for more than two years in a row, was
               always on my butt for not having goals.

David winds up and throws the basketball at the backboard. It's a long throw and he misses.

                    MARY
               You said your dad used to play ball...

David doesn't answer.

                    MARY (CONT'D)
               Is that why you want a championship
               jacket? Goals? Get him back?

This hits a little too close to home.

                    DAVID
               Do you always ask exactly what you're
               thinking?

Mary smiles.

                    DAVID (CONT'D)
               Well, I don't want him back.

There is a moment of silence as they both digest this. They begin to swing again, softly.

                    MARY
               But you don't want to be the reason why
               he left either.

David just looks at her. She's right.

                    DAVID
          He thinks I'm worthless. That's why he
          left. I'm not doing this for him and I
          don't want him back but I am gonna
          prove myself – on his terms.
                    (pause)
          Is that stupid?

                    MARY
          Well, I don't know about a championship
          jacket...
                    (from her depths)
          ...but I know what you mean about not
          wanting to feel worthless.

INT. LAKESHORE HIGH GYM - NIGHT

A junior varsity game has just finished. It will be about another half an hour before the varsity begins. The JV game hasn't attracted much of a crowd and people are still filing in for the main attraction.

In between games, Dribbles is unintentionally entertaining the fans.

He's taken a basketball out of a large net bag and is shooting diaper shots out on the empty court. A small pep-band in the bleachers plays to his antics.

Eddie, dressed in street clothes, is standing over near the doors, watching Dribbles with contempt.

A group of cheerleaders, some in uniform, some in street clothes, walks in behind Eddie and sets down a large, wooden, run-through frame with paper stretched across it. On the paper is painted a large "L."

                    EDDIE
            (still watching Dribbles)
    Retard.

Eddie looks down in disgust and sees the large net bag full of basketballs. Beside the bag, leaning against the wall, is Dribbles' broom.

Eddie looks around to see if anyone is paying attention to him. They aren't. The crowd is too busy giggling at Dribbles' antics out on the court.

Beside the paper run-through the girls have made for the team, is a box with large ink markers in it. Eddie grabs these markers just as David comes walking into the gym, heading for the locker room.

                    EDDIE (CONT'D)
    McNeil!

David cautiously approaches him.

                    EDDIE (CONT'D)
            Christian tells me you're an artist.

                    DAVID
            I draw and paint some.

                    EDDIE
            I need you to do something for me. For a
            joke...
                    (pause)
            ...a good joke.

David starts to walk away.

                    EDDIE (CONT'D)
            On Dribbles.

David stops. Eddie hands David the markers.

The crowd lets out a BURST OF LAUGHTER.

Dribbles, out on the court, is still trying to shoot diaper shots. He's not joking around, he's serious. The laughter from the crowd is upsetting him.

INT. LAKESHORE HIGH, LOCKER ROOM - NIGHT

Eddie slips into the locker room carrying the broom handle on which he has fastened the net bag. Some of the team members see him enter and they come over to him.

> CHRISTIAN
> Hey, hey!

> MICHAUD
> Don't let Stephan catch you in here. You only got one more game of suspension.

> CHRISTIAN
> (eying the broom handle and bag)
> What's that?

> EDDIE
> I need a favor.

No one responds. Eddie eyes their white warm-up trousers and jackets. The white jackets have stripes and numbers on the outside.

> EDDIE (CONT'D)
> Turn your jackets inside-out...

The other players look at him questioningly.

INT. LAKESHORE HIGH GYM - NIGHT

David is drawing something on the paper run-through the cheerleaders have made.

Eddie comes out of the locker room, wearing a white jacket and carrying his make-shift net.

He looks into the athletic office.

INT. LAKESHORE HIGH, ATHLETIC OFFICE - NIGHT

Stephan sits at his desk, going over the stats of the team they will play tonight.

INT. LAKESHORE HIGH GYM - NIGHT

Eddie leads Christian and two other players out near the edge of the court, where David has finished drawing on the paper run-through.

Eddie has David and one of the players hold up the run-through, facing the court.

David has added to the large "L." The run-through now reads, "Loony Brigade."

Dribbles continues to throw diaper shots, ignoring the crowd.

Eddie signals the pep band. They think the team is about ready to take the court. They begin PLAYING AN ENERGETIC CHARGE. Also in the bleachers, Mary looks curiously over to David, standing and holding the run-through.

INT. LAKESHORE HIGH ATHLETIC OFFICE - NIGHT

Stephan hears the pep band playing the charge and rises to see what the commotion is all about.

INT. LAKESHORE HIGH GYM - NIGHT

Eddie, Michaud and another player come crashing through the run-through. Eddie is carrying the make-shift net.

The crowd, thinking they are coming out for warm-ups, begins cheering.

Dribbles, unsure of what's going on, stops shooting and holds his basketball to his chest.

As Eddie and the others run toward him, he awkwardly backs away, and then begins to run away.

Eddie swings the net and catches Dribbles in it.

Some of the crowd breaks into LAUGHTER.

Mary, watching this scene, is definitely not laughing. She's furious. She looks over court-side to see...

David, still holding the side of the run-through, is laughing.

Eddie and the two other players in their white jackets and net drag Dribbles across the court.

David is still laughing as they drag Dribbles over near him.

Stephan arrives and is trying to sort out what's happening.

A KID IN THE CROWD, near the edge of the bleachers, yells out.

> KID IN CROWD
> Hey look! He pissed himself!

David's laughter stops and his grin disappears.

A fresh, dark stain is in the crotch of Dribbles' pants. David sees that the old man is trembling and crying.

The color drains from David's face. He lets go of the run-through and it falls to the floor. With the LAUGHTER OF OTHERS still ringing in his ears, he is so disgusted with himself and rocked that he has to back up a step and lean against the bleachers for support.

EXT. LAKESHORE HIGH - NIGHT

The game is over. People are heading for their cars. A few kids hang around in the parking lot and WHOOP and HOLLER.

EXT. STREETS OF LAKESHORE - NIGHT

Mary's still fuming, sitting way over on the passenger side of the front seat.

As David drives, he looks like he's about to fall apart. The tough defensive shell he has been building since his father left has finally crumbled under its own weight.

>   DAVID
>   (near tears)
>   I am sorry.
>
>   MARY
>   Telling me doesn't do any good.
>
>   DAVID
>   Sometimes I have trouble thinking of
>   other people as being – real.
>
>   MARY
>   You emotionally tortured that poor man.
>   What did he ever do to you?

David takes Mary's rhetorical question seriously and reflects on it.

>   DAVID
>   (surprised at himself)
>   He embarrassed me...

Mary glares at him.

>   DAVID (CONT'D)
>   It embarrassed me to be around him – to
>   have other people think I was with him.
>   (mad at himself)
>   So I showed everyone what a man I was,
>   and how much better than him I am, by
>   treating him like crap.

MARY
          Didn't you think at all? Obviously he has
          some problems – didn't you wonder how
          he might feel?

                    DAVID
          No, I didn't.

David slows the car.

                    MARY
          What...?

He pulls over.

EXT. LAKESHORE STREET - NIGHT

Dribbles is at the side of the road. He's got a flat tire on his bike.

David gets out of the car.

                    DAVID
          Can I help?

Dribbles backs up a step.

                    DAVID (CONT'D)
          I'm sorry, I want to help.

Mary rolls her window down.

                    MARY
          It's O.K., he means it. He's a jerk, but
          he's an honest jerk.

                    DAVID
          Thanks.

Dribbles seems to believe this. He looks around the empty street. He doesn't have much choice.

INT. DRIBBLES' APARTMENT - NIGHT

Dribbles unlocks the door to his apartment and enters, followed by Mary and then David carrying the bike.

Dribbles turns on a light and David sets the bike down.

> DRIBBLES
> Thank you.

> DAVID
> Look, I just wanted to say I was sorry
> again for... whoa!

David has just gotten a load of Dribbles' apartment. Though it is run-down and filthy, it is filled with Lakeshore Lancers basketball memorabilia dating back to the thirties. One wall is covered with team photos.

Signed game balls sit on a bookshelf.

Scrapbooks filled with newspaper clippings are on the coffee table.

An entire backboard, rim and net are mounted to another wall. The backboard is signed with autographs to Dribbles from the team members of the 1967 State Championship team.

In the center of the room, a battered 8mm movie projector and screen are set up. And in a display case, are examples of the various styles of Lancers' uniforms from over the years.

David and Mary walk around the room examining the artifacts.

Mary stares at the backboard.

> DRIBBLES
> Down that one came when the glass ones
> went up.

David and Mary make their way over to the display case with the uniforms. In the case with the uniforms is a state championship, letter-man's jacket and a trophy.

David is transfixed by the jacket. He reads the sleeve: "1985 State Champs - Dribbles Stedman."

> MARY
> You were on the 1985 Lancers?

David elbows her and points to a PHOTO OF A TEAM OF YOUNG MEN PRESENTING DRIBBLES WITH A JACKET. It is quite clear in the photo that Dribbles was not a part of this team – he wears his custodian's uniform and, though younger in this photo, is still not close to the age of playing high school basketball.

David stares intently at the photo as we notice the same young man from the photo in David's room is also in the group of players in this photo.

> DAVID
> My dad was on that team.

> DRIBBLES
> (matter of fact)
> Alex McNeil.

David's caught off guard by this.

> DRIBBLES (CONT'D)
> Point guard, number 52.

> DAVID
> That's right, how did you...?

Dribbles has walked out of the room.

> MARY
> The 1985 Lancers?

> DAVID
> It was a really big deal. Lakeshore played up a class, you know, for the size of the schools. They won the championship by beating a school four times their size.

> MARY
> Must've been really good.

> DAVID
> I guess.

Dribbles re-enters the room. He's carrying a shoe-box. He gives it to David.

David finds the box full of reels of Super 8mm film. On the side of the box, written in black marker is, "Lancers 1985."

                    MARY
          Hey, isn't that when you said...?

David's emotions are confused. He's almost angry.

                    DAVID
          ...my father played. I don't have time to
          sit and watch these now.

                    DRIBBLES
          Take 'em with you.

                    DAVID
          Take them?

                    MARY
          What if something happens?

                    DRIBBLES
              (as though talking to a
               child)
          You could be real careful with them.

INT. MCNEIL HOUSE, LIVING ROOM - NIGHT

Sarah is sitting up on the couch, struggling with the checkbook again. The headlights from an outside car sweep across the wall.

Moments later, David comes quietly in, carrying his shoe box.

                    SARAH
          I am not waiting up because I'm worried
          about my car.

                    DAVID
              (pleasantly)
          Hey, Mom.

She hasn't heard this tone from him in a while and it's refreshing for her.

                    SARAH
          Well, hey there yourself.

                    DAVID
              (walking out of the
                     room)
              How was your day?

                    SARAH
              (she shrugs/to herself)
              Not bad, not bad.

INT. MCNEIL HOUSE, ATTIC - NIGHT

David aims his flashlight and rummages through assorted junk packed in boxes. The dust he blows from coverings fills the air, creating a soft atmosphere in the attic and defining the moonlight which streams in through the small, round window. Pulling a cylindrical tin can out of one box, David at first starts to throw it aside but then thinks better of it and stops. He examines the tin more closely. It is a bicycle tire patch kit.

David stuffs this tin in his back pocket and continues searching. He finds a two foot cube, plastic box.

Propping the flashlight between his knees, he wipes off the dust and presses the release latch on the door on the box. A vintage Super 8mm projector, in pristine condition, sits inside.

INT. MCNEIL HOUSE, DAVID'S ROOM - NIGHT

Black. The HUM OF AN OLD ELECTRIC MOTOR TRANSFORMER, and the RHYTHMIC METALLIC CHATTER of precision gears and sprockets breaks the silence. A focused beam of light issues from the projector lens and slices through the darkness.

The familiar white leader with the red Kodak stripe, now yellowing from age, dances on the wall of David's room. It is replaced by the bright, splotchy colors of overexposed frames, then the jittering, grainy, Super 8mm image of boys playing basketball.

David's face is intent as it is illuminated by the pulsing glow of light being reflected from the wall.

EXT. DRIBBLES' APARTMENT BUILDING - DAY

The Caprice pulls over to the side of the road and parks in front of Dribbles' building.

INT. CAPRICE - DAY

Sarah is driving. David, carrying his books and tire patch kit, hops out of the car.

>   DAVID
>   This is it. Thanks.
>
>   SARAH
>   Who lives here?

She is too late. David is off toward the building. She pulls away.

INT. DRIBBLES' APARTMENT - DAY

Dribbles makes his way to the door as David knocks.

EXT. DRIBBLES' APARTMENT - DAY

As Dribbles opens the door, David holds up the tire patch kit and smiles.

EXT. STREETS OF LAKESHORE - DAY

A bicycle wobbles down the side of the street on the crisp November morning. Dribbles is riding David on the back of the bike. David is sitting on a narrow carry-all rack above the rear fender. His legs dangle off to the sides of the wheel and his feet drag on the ground. Their breaths puff out white in the cold air and their faces are red. The strain on a man of Dribbles' age, riding two on a bike, is obvious, but he rides every day, is in good shape, and seems to be enjoying himself.

David, however, is getting rattled. His teeth chatter and he grips the carry-all trying in vain to shift his weight to his palms from his groin.

                    DAVID
                (voice vibrating)
            Y-Y-You-ou s-s-sure y-y-you d-d-don't w-
            w-want m-me t-t-t-to p-p-pedal?

Dribbles turns back to look at David, smiles and shakes his head no.

Not watching where he's going, Dribbles heads straight for a pot-hole. David sees it.

                    DAVID (CONT'D)
            H-H-H-H-Hey!

The bike smacks right into the pot-hole. David's groin racks into the carry-all. He screams.

Dribbles keeps pedaling and looks to the tires.

                    DRIBBLES
            Hey, hey. The tire's still goody goody
            good.

                    DAVID
            W-W-Wish I c-could s-s-s-say the s-s-s-
            same for my nutsy, nutsy, nuts!

INT. LAKESHORE HIGH, HALLWAY - DAY

The hallway is alive as students arrive and socialize at their lockers. Dribbles is busy with a rag and cleanser, wiping an obscenity off the side of one row of lockers.

Finishing his job, he turns to get a drink of water from a fountain but he freezes.

Eddie is just down the hall a short way from him. Hanging up his coat and taking books out of his locker, Eddie talks to his girlfriend, Sheri. Sheri's eyes are red and puffy. Dribbles pulls back, so as not to be seen, behind a couple of girls chatting at their lockers. He pretends to continue wiping the spot he has already cleaned. Sheri, visibly upset, wipes her eyes and storms away. Eddie SLAMS his LOCKER DOOR LOUDLY.

The locker girls in front of Dribbles are startled, then hush.

> LOCKER GIRL #1
> (under her breath/about Eddie)
> What's his problem?

> LOCKER GIRL #2
> You don't know?

Dribbles turns his attention to this exchange.

Locker Girl #2 surreptitiously cradles her arms, rocks them, and HUMS A LULLABY.

> LOCKER GIRL #1
> Sheri?

Locker Girl #2 sadly nods in the affirmative. A BELL RINGS. The crowd dissipates, leaving only Dribbles, staring at Eddie.

Eddie is lost in his own thoughts, staring at the floor. He finally looks up and sees Dribbles. A moment of tension hangs between the two of them, alone in the hallway.

A second BELL RINGS, they both walk off in opposite directions.

A DOOR SLAMS in the hallway and ECHOES. Empty and silent for a moment, the hall is suddenly filled with the RASPING REVERBERATING VOICE of the ANNOUNCER (HARVE).

> HARVE (V.O.)
> We'd like to welcome back the Lancers' leading scorer, Eddd-eeeee... Cooooooooooles!

A CROWD ROARS in approval.

DISSOLVE TO:

INT. LAKESHORE HIGH GYM - NIGHT

Eddie, in his warm-ups, runs out from court-side to join the rest of the team who are already out loosening up.

At the bench, David gets his charts in order.

Dribbles makes some adjustments on the lens of his VHS camera. Holding it up to his face, he points the camera toward the court to adjust the focus.

Suddenly, he pulls the camera down and glares toward the court.

The Lancers have formed two rows in front of the basket and are doing lay-ups. Eddie, however, is not paying attention. He is staring over toward the bench – at Dribbles.

A BUZZER SOUNDS.

The Lancers halt their lay-ups and head for the bench. The basketballs bounce and roll loosely around the court. Only Eddie holds onto his ball.

A couple of the loose balls roll over to the bench and bounce off the chairs. David ignores them and continues to work on his charts.

> DAVID
> (to Dribbles)
> Can you get those? I'm behind here.

As the players arrive at the bench, Dribbles sets down his camera and gathers the balls into the net bag. Eddie walks to the bench, carrying a basketball and before huddling up, he rudely pushes the ball into Dribbles' chest. They exchange a glance.

Eddie huddles up.

Dribbles stares at the ball he is holding.

                        STEPHAN
            Michaud, you'll be starting instead of
            Dwight. Christian, all over fifteen. Don't
            give up a shot, make him pass. Eddie...

A RIPPLE OF LAUGHTER passes through the crowd. Stephan and the players look around to see what's so funny.

Dribbles is prancing back and forth in front of the scorer's table. He has taken Eddie's basketball and stuffed it under his sweatshirt, making himself look pregnant.

The crowd laughs at Dribbles' antics, most of them not understanding the significance of what he's doing.

Dribbles and Eddie make eye contact.

Eddie makes a break toward Dribbles.

Dribbles runs, the ball bouncing under his shirt.

The crowd stops laughing.

A REFEREE grabs Eddie by the arm. Seconds later, Christian and Michaud are there, holding Eddie back, calming him.

In the bleachers, in the middle of a group of her friends, Sheri is humiliated. Most people who know her and Eddie have just made the connection and they turn to stare at her.

Her eyes tear up. A friend who already knew, puts an arm around her shoulder to comfort her.

Christian and Michaud bring Eddie back to the bench.

Dribbles has stopped near the edge of the bleachers and the locker room. He watches the action. He looks up to the bleachers and scans the crowd. His eyes focus on something.

Sheri, still being comforted by her friends, is crying.

Dribbles takes the ball out from under his shirt, disgusted. Like David, he didn't count on innocent victims.

DISSOLVE TO:

EXT. LAKESHORE HIGH GYM DOORS - NIGHT

A CLOSE-UP of a streetlight shows that the first snow of the season has started. The storm is incredible. The air is dead, with not so much as a hint of breeze, but the snowflakes – the snowflakes are enormous.

Actually, what are falling, aren't really flakes at all, but two-inch wafers of clustered flakes. They fill the sky and drift lazily to the ground in the still night.

Disturbing the peace of this scene, a BUS ROARS into the frame and HUFFS to a stop. A gym door opens, we see the bleachers are just about empty and the game is over. Dribbles walks out into the night, looking up at the streetlight and the snow. He raises his camera and tapes this beautiful sight. The BUS DRIVER steps outside and also looks up, in awe.

                        BUS DRIVER
        Biggest damn snowflakes I ever saw.
        What the heck you call them?

>   DRIBBLES
>   (stops taping)
>   Not snow, Manna.

The bus driver looks at him curiously.

>   DRIBBLES (CONT'D)
>   From Heaven.

INT. LAKESHORE HIGH, TEAM ROOM - NIGHT

David sits alone in the team room. He also looks hot. He drinks a squirt of water from the plastic bottle. He totals his charts. SLAMMING LOCKER DOORS and the VOICES OF THE TEAM can be heard drifting in from the locker room. David takes another hit of water, puts down his charts, and heads for the door leading outside.

EXT. LAKESHORE HIGH TEAM ROOM DOOR - NIGHT

David steps outside of the team room with no coat on and he takes a lung-full of the cool air. Giant snowflakes powder his hair and shoulders. His breath is visible when he exhales but the air is refreshing rather than chilling.

David is around the corner from where the buses arrive.

EXT. LAKESHORE HIGH GYM DOORS - NIGHT

Dribbles and the bus driver still stand just outside the gym doors. The driver is in his shirt-sleeves. They're both still amazed by the snow.

>   BUS DRIVER
>   God, that's beautiful. Makes everything
>   seem so gentle and – peaceful, ya know.
>   Nobody could have any troubles on a
>   night like tonight.

The bus driver shivers a little. He heads into the bus to get a jacket. Bringing his camera to his face once again, Dribbles films the sky.

The POINT OF VIEW of the VHS view-finder is somehow beautiful in grainy black and white. The streetlight Dribbles points at creates lens flares through which the snowflakes dance.

Suddenly, the SCREEN GOES BLACK.

We then see Eddie has crept up and pulled the camera away from Dribbles' face by the lens. His other hand is over Dribbles' mouth as he drags him toward the corner of the gym.

Dribbles gets his hand with the camera free and tries to swing it, but Eddie slaps his hand away roughly. The camera sails off into the night.

EXT. LAKESHORE HIGH TEAM ROOM DOOR - NIGHT

David is about to turn and go back into the team room when something bounces and skids along the sidewalk near him.

He investigates and finds Dribbles' camera, smashed. Bending down to pick up the camera, he's startled by the commotion as Eddie drags Dribbles around the corner of the gym. Eddie, wild-eyed, sees David and freezes. David slowly rises. Dribbles weakly struggles like a small child.

> EDDIE
> (shaky)
> Get out of here, David!

David instinctively backs off, then stops.

> DAVID
> (weakly)
> He didn't do anything...

Eddie's eyes have the sparkle of madness.

> EDDIE
> You wanna be next?

David looks from Eddie to Dribbles. The old man's cap is pushed down onto his forehead. His face is distorted from Eddie's tight grip over his mouth. His eyes are pleading.

David holds his gaze for a moment that hangs like an eternity.

                    EDDIE (CONT'D)
        Swear to God, McNeil!

David hesitates, then turns and runs back into the team room.

INT. LAKESHORE HIGH, TEAM ROOM - NIGHT

David bursts into the room, shaken, closes the door, and leans against it as though he would fall without it. His strength has drained from him. There is the OFF-SCREEN SOUND of a HARD BLOW TO THE BODY followed by a MUFFLED CRY from Dribbles.

David bangs his head against the door in frustration.

Another BLOW and MUFFLED CRY. David begins banging his head rhythmically. Mary bursts into the team room.

                    MARY
        Here you are. Everybody else is...

When David sees her, shame covers his face like a mask.

                    MARY (CONT'D)
        What...?

David pumps himself up, grabs the doorknob and shouts at her.

                    DAVID
        Stay here!

EXT. LAKESHORE HIGH TEAM ROOM DOOR - NIGHT

Eddie has Dribbles up against the wall and is hammering him with body blows. He no longer holds a hand over the old man's mouth.

He doesn't have to – Dribbles no longer has any breath with which to scream. As Eddie pummels him, what comes out of Dribbles' mouth is something like a convulsive wretch.

David charges up behind Eddie, but Eddie has seen him out of the corner of his eye. As the two of them meet, Eddie wheels, grabs David by the shoulders and lifts a knee into his groin.

David's air rushes out of him as he turns, staggers, and falls on the thin coating of snow on the side-walk.

> EDDIE
> I told you, man, I TOLD YOU!

David's breath comes in rapid gasps, as he tries shaking off the pain. Mary steps out of the doorway and she and Eddie lock their gazes on one another until Mary turns and runs into the building.

A soft moan escapes Dribbles. Eddie starts toward him when he is suddenly tackled from behind by David. Rolling around in the snow, Eddie is trying to squirm out of the hug that David has around his waist.

> DAVID
> Leave him alone!

Eddie starts whaling on David's back. He too, looks on the verge of tears.

> EDDIE
> (wildly, while beating on
> David)
> It's a joke to everybody, right? Well,
> we're gonna have that kid! We're gonna
> have it!

Mary, Stephan, and the bus driver come running around the corner. Stephan and the bus driver pull David and Eddie apart while Mary runs over to Dribbles.

Helping Dribbles to his feet, Mary doesn't like the way he looks. She gets him standing against the wall. He's holding his stomach area and his eyes don't focus on anything.

> MARY
> I think he needs a doctor.

On the word "doctor," Dribbles reacts violently.

                    STEPHAN
            Phone's in the athletic office.

                    DRIBBLES
                    (slurred)
            No doctor. Uh-unh. Uh-unh. UH-
            UNH. No. No. NO!

                    MARY
            You O.K.?

Still in pain, looking up in the direction of a streetlight, Dribbles speech is slightly better.

                    DRIBBLES
            Okee Dokee smokee.

From Dribbles' POINT OF VIEW, we see the streetlight. The snow is petering out.

                    DRIBBLES (O.S.) (CONT'D)
                    (weakly)
            Okee Dokee.

EXT. MCNEIL HOUSE - NIGHT

Christian's car cruises down the street. Here and there a few houses have on colored Christmas lights.

Pulling over to the side of the street and getting out of his car, Christian pauses a moment to look at the lights before heading up to David's house.

INT. MCNEIL HOUSE, DAVID'S ROOM - NIGHT

Drawing paper sprawled out all over his bed, David is plugged into his inexpensive stereo through headphones and drawing.

Judging by the large number of papers that have been crumpled, whatever he is drawing isn't coming out to his satisfaction.

There is a KNOCK AT THE DOOR, but it cannot penetrate the teenager's headphones.

As the CAMERA WORKS CLOSER to David, we see that his sketches are of Mary.

The KNOCK AT THE DOOR is louder, still no response from David. Christian enters and this David does see. He tries to look casual while shuffling his drawings together into one stack and covering them with the pad.

> CHRISTIAN
> Your new room, huh?

> DAVID
> (pulling off headsets)
> Huh?

Christian has something he wants to say – he hedges.

> CHRISTIAN
> I haven't really seen you drawing anything since you went out for the team.

David makes sure the drawings are well covered by the pad.

> DAVID
> Well, you know...

> CHRISTIAN
> You heard Eddie's kicked off the team.

> DAVID
> Want an apology from me?

> CHRISTIAN
> Apology?

> DAVID
> You know. Isn't that why you came here? To tell me about Eddie? How it's my fault? How I got the big star kicked off the team?

Christian is taken aback. He didn't expect this outburst.

CHRISTIAN
I came to see if you were O.K. To see if
things were O.K. between you and me.
(pause)
I guess I got my answer.

DAVID
Right.

Christian heads for the door, stops, and considers. He tries one more time.

CHRISTIAN
Eddie did a screwed-up thing.

David glares at him.

CHRISTIAN (CONT'D)
He did A LOT of screwed-up things,
O.K.? But the guy was under incredible
pressure.

DAVID
And that makes it O.K.?

CHRISTIAN
No. No it doesn't.
(pause)
But sometimes pressure can make a guy
do some stupid things – REALLY stupid
things. That doesn't always necessarily
make him some kind of asshole.

DAVID
It usually does.

CHRISTIAN
But not always. You should know that.

David stops to think about this.

CHRISTIAN (CONT'D)
I just want our friendship back.

INT. LAKESHORE HIGH, HALLWAY - DAY

A BELL RINGS. Classroom doors open and students spill into the hallway.

INT. LAKESHORE HIGH, DAN STEPHAN'S CLASSROOM - DAY

David and Mary are among the last students heading for the door. Before they can get there...

>   STEPHAN
>   McNeil.

Hanging behind and letting the crowd leave, David motions for Mary to go on ahead. He goes over to the coach.

>   STEPHAN (CONT'D)
>   You heard about Coles?

David nods.

>   STEPHAN (CONT'D)
>   That leaves me with a spot open.
>   (pause)
>   You weren't the next best guy. You know
>   that. There were a couple of guys better,
>   but I thought all things considered...

Stephan is waiting for David to jump on this, and when he doesn't, the coach is surprised.

>   STEPHAN (CONT'D)
>   You interested or what?

>   DAVID
>   (confidence rather than
>   excitement)
>   Yeah.

>   STEPHAN
>   Don't tell me that fire in your belly's
>   burned out.

David does not respond.

                    STEPHAN (CONT'D)
          Don't expect much. You won't be in
          Coles' position. You may not even see
          any court time.

                    DAVID
          I get a uniform?

                    STEPHAN
          I could paint a number on your cup...

EXT. CRYSTAL LAKE, PARKING LOT - NIGHT

Snow covers the ground, and save for the Caprice, the parking lot is empty.

INT. CAPRICE - NIGHT

David and Mary lay in urgent cramped passion in the front seat. The awkwardness of the encounter adds heat for David. Mary is uncomfortable – physically and spiritually. The two are at the stage of deep kissing. David's hands are curious and eager. The key is in the "ACC" position and the radio fans the flames. Instead of a typical teen torch song, however, a CHRISTMAS LOVE BALLAD IS PLAYING.

David pulls Mary's sweater up over her head. Her hair, usually meticulously groomed, falls wildly down over her face, neck, and bare shoulders. She swipes the hair away with her hand and a few curled strands cling to the light film of sweat on her forehead.

David kisses her again and slips the shoulder straps of her bra down over her arms. He unbuttons his shirt.

Mary suddenly writhes and digs the cold, chrome seat-belt buckle out from under her bare back. She fixes her bra.

                    MARY
          David, turn the heat on please, I'm cold.

He does not want to be interrupted.

                    DAVID
          Carbon monoxide in an idling car. I
          can't...

Mary works her way out from under him and gropes for her sweater.

                    MARY
          Then I have to put my sweater on.

Like a shot.

                    DAVID
          Wait, wait. I'll start the car.

David goes for the ignition.

                    DAVID (CONT'D)
          We can open the windows a crack.

                    MARY
                (putting on her sweater)
          No.

David stops and looks at her.

                    MARY (CONT'D)
          I mean, yes, go ahead and start the car but
          no, I don't know if this is right.
                (pause)
          I mean I don't know how you feel about
          me. What are you thinking?

David is a little embarrassed but defensive at the same time.

                    DAVID
          Well, what are YOU thinking?

                    MARY
          I'm thinking I'd like to get to know David
          McNeil better.
                (pause)
          Wanna go for a walk?

                    DAVID
          I thought you were cold?

EXT. CRYSTAL LAKE, ROADSIDE - NIGHT

Although they have coats on, David and Mary keep their arms around one another for warmth as they walk along.

The road is heavily wooded on one side but open to the lake on the other. Everything except for the water is covered in a fresh coating of snow and the light from the almost full moon casts a cool, bluish glow over the landscape.

                    MARY
          I do like you, it's just that, I'm scared, you
          know?
                    (pause)
          I don't want to end up like Eddie and
          Sheri. I'm not ready for that yet.

David is a little surprised at this.

                    DAVID
          Just what did you think was going to
          happen tonight?

                    MARY
          Seemed pretty obvious to me.

                    DAVID
          Just so you'll know, I'm not ready for that
          either.

                    MARY
          Where were we going then?

                    DAVID
          I don't know.
                    (pause)
          I know what you CAN do and what you
          CAN'T do but it's the in-between that
          gets me confused.

                    MARY
          How close can you come to what you
          can't do and still feel right about it? The
          "Gray Area."

                    DAVID
          I feel that way all the time.

                    MARY
                  (shocked)
          ALL the time!

David laughs. That's not what he meant.

                    DAVID
          No, not THAT way. I feel like what you
          said about the gray area. I know what's
          right and I know what's wrong, but
          sometimes the in-between...

He shrugs.

                    MARY
          I think you pretty much have to go with
          your instincts, you know. It's like people
          have voices telling them what to do in
          different situations. And they have
          reasons for acting one way or another...
                  (pause)
          But deep down inside I think everyone
          knows which voice is right and which is
          wrong and it's just a matter of making up
          your mind who you're going to listen to.

She laughs.

                    DAVID
          What?

                    MARY
          I know it'll sound stupid, sometimes
          when I don't know what to do, I imagine
          that I'm the heroine of a novel or a movie
          and then I put myself in the audience and
          ask myself, "If I were reading this book,
          or watching this movie, what would I
          want me to do?"
                    (pause)
          And that's what I do.

David gives her a look.

                    MARY (CONT'D)
                    (laughing)
          Well, O.K., not always...

                    DAVID
          Do you think that someone can do
          something that seems like a rotten thing
          to everyone, but really, inside, they were
          listening to their "good" voice?

                    MARY
          Sure, I think so.

INT. MCNEIL HOUSE, DAVID'S ROOM - NIGHT

A grainy, pulsing image of David's father dances across the wall. The young man in the film bears a strong resemblance to David but is more athletic.

David's father wears number fifty-two and plays guard. The film David is projecting was shot in the Lancers' gym. The gym doesn't seem to have changed much since 1985, only the fashion and hair styles of the students.

ON FILM, David's father puts up a jump shot and scores. The crowd reacts wildly.

Running back down-court, the young man holds up one finger to the crowd to signify that they are number one. The image of David's father freezes. David has switched the projector to the STILL FRAME mode. He has a pad of paper and pencil on his lap and he studies the scene on the wall intently – then begins to sketch.

Suddenly, the image on the wall is washed out in a flood of light as David's mother cautiously opens the door to the hallway.

>   SARAH
>   (peering into the
>   darkened room)
>   David?

David quickly turns the projector off.

>   SARAH (CONT'D)
>   (smiling)
>   What on earth are you doing with your
>   grandfather's old movie projector?

>   DAVID
>   Nothing.

Sarah's smile fades.

>   SARAH
>   What are you watching? Are those dirty
>   movies?

>   DAVID
>   I'm not watching dirty movies.

>   SARAH
>   I want to see that film.

>   DAVID
>   It's NOT a dirty movie!

>   SARAH
>   Run it!

David clicks on the projector.

>   DAVID
>   Close the door.

David's father once again runs down the court, signaling to the crowd. Sarah sucks in a breath.

SARAH
OH – MY – GOD. Where'd you get
this?

DAVID
That guy, Dribbles – he gave me a whole
box of them.

She hasn't heard a word.

SARAH
Look at him! He's just a kid, ready to
beat the world. Home whites 52.
(pause)
Were we really that young? I almost
forgot.

The image disappears in darkness. David has shut down the projector.

DAVID
Give it a few more years, maybe we can
forget what he looked like altogether.

Sarah is brought rudely back to the present by this remark.

SARAH
O.K., O.K. I guess maybe it is high time
we had a talk. I know you're angry at
your father for leaving. I understand
that...

DAVID
(incredulous)
Angry? I'm pissed off! Not for leaving
either. For NEVER being here in the
first place.

Sarah looks confused.

DAVID (CONT'D)
Poor David, Dad ran away and he hasn't
had a father for six months.
(pause)
Well, I got news for you. I never HAD a
father...

> SARAH
> Is that what you think? Your daddy neglected you? Your daddy didn't take you to ball games? Your daddy didn't take you fishing? Well, I got news for YOU, son, your daddy was working three jobs to keep the bills paid.

Sarah takes a moment to compose herself.

> SARAH (CONT'D)
> I know you can count and figure out your father and I were only seventeen when you were born, so I guess it's kind of obvious you weren't exactly a planned pregnancy...

This is no revelation to David. He actually sees some humor in it.

> DAVID
> David McNeil – "love child."

> SARAH
> I'm glad you think it's funny now. I can tell you no one was laughing then. We were just out of high school and your dad had a basketball scholarship to college...

> DAVID
> He had to marry you...

                    SARAH
          No he didn't. I told him to go. HE said,
          "No way."

David is uncomfortable in this conversation but his need to know is great.

                    DAVID
          You were gonna get an abortion?

                    SARAH
          No! Your grandmother and grandfather
          had agreed to help me raise you.
                    (pause)
          Your father stayed because he wanted to.

Inside, David has always desperately wanted a reason to like his father, but now that the information is beginning to come, he resists it. He switches the projector back on and both of them are illuminated by its glow.

                    DAVID
          Maybe he stayed because he was scared of
          going off. Maybe I was a convenient
          excuse.

SARAH
I thought that for a while too. But it wasn't true. We loved each other, but neither one of us wanted to stay together and raise a family.
(pause)
The only thing he wanted more than taking off, was doing the right thing. Problem was, the right thing for you wasn't the right thing for him. You wanna hear some irony? Working sixty hours a week, he never got to know you, you resented him – and you were the whole reason he stayed in the first place.

David is angry and confused.

DAVID
So what happened? He get tired of playing martyr?

SARAH
This is the hard part, David. For me anyway. He didn't walk out on us...
(pause)
I told him to leave.

David doesn't know where to focus his emotions.

SARAH (CONT'D)
He wasn't doing you any good. He was barely doing me any good. And we were destroying him.

She breaks down.

                    SARAH (CONT'D)
          When your grandparents moved and
          there was room is this house, I knew we
          could get by, just the two of us.
                    (pause)
          I may have made a mistake. If I did, I'm
          sorry. But I wouldn't have done it if I
          didn't think it would be better for
          everyone.

INT. LAKESHORE HIGH, ATHLETIC OFFICE - DAY

Joiner is in a large walk-in closet. He is stacking cardboard boxes on a shelf when David enters.

                    JOINER
          Hey, congratulations kid. Sure hope
          Stephan knows what the hell he's doing.

David is not taking any of this.

                    DAVID
          Where are the uniforms?

Joiner motions to three boxes sitting on the floor. The boxes are labeled "00-19, 20-39, 40-60."

                    JOINER
          You want small, forty to sixty.

Joiner goes for the box. He rummages through it and comes out with two uniforms, one light and one dark – number forty-eight.

David looks past these, into the box.

                    DAVID
          Fifty-two still in there?

INT. MCNEIL HOUSE, LIVING ROOM - CHRISTMAS DAY

David and Mary sit on a sofa while Sarah walks around straightening up the room a little. A small, decorated, Christmas tree stands in the corner.

Under the tree are about ten presents, already unwrapped. Most of the presents are simple and practical, such as items of clothing. Mary motions to a smaller box though, that contains artist's brushes.

> MARY
> Whose are those?

> DAVID
> Mom got me those and she shouldn't have because they're real expensive...

> SARAH
> Well, you just forget about that, because it's worth it to me as long as they get used.

> DAVID
> (to Mary)
> I've got this really nice paint box, but the brushes in it are getting kind of beat.
> (pause/sniffs the air)
> What is that great smell? What're you cooking?

> SARAH
> Not me.

David and Mary look at each other and smile.

> DAVID
> Annie?

> SARAH
> Uh-huh. Christmas turkey.

> DAVID
> What? From Swanson?

Annie has appeared in the doorway.

> ANNIE
> I heard that. Now everybody in the dining room so Annie can give you the bird.

As they all head for the dining room, David whispers to Mary.

                    DAVID
          This may not be a pretty sight.

INT. MCNEIL HOUSE, DINING ROOM - CHRISTMAS DAY

The dining room looks great. Everyone except Annie is shocked – especially David.

The table, with the turkey and all the trimmings, is right out of a Norman Rockwell painting.

                    SARAH
          This is so great!

The others nod in agreement. They walk around and take seats at the table.

Mary notices something strange. The traditional paper crowns covering the ends of the drumsticks are embellished with rhinestones.

                    ANNIE
          Ain't they something? I came up with
          that idea.

                    MARY
          They're really nice.

                    DAVID
          This is great, Annie. It's like what
          everyone should have for Christmas.

EXT. DRIBBLES' APARTMENT BUILDING - NIGHT

Sarah's car pulls over and parks.

INT. CAPRICE - NIGHT

David is driving. Mary sits on the passenger side holding several heaping plates of food covered with aluminum foil. She goes to get out of the car.

> MARY
> This was a super idea.

> DAVID
> Hold on a second.

He pulls a small, gift-wrapped package out from under his coat and hands it to her.

> MARY
> We said we weren't getting each other anything...

David shrugs. Mary opens the package. In it are a hard cover book with empty pages and a blank VHS cassette. Mary looks puzzled.

> DAVID
> So you can make yourself the heroine of your own novel and movie and always know what the right thing to do is.

She smiles and kisses him.

INT. DRIBBLES' APARTMENT - NIGHT

Dribbles looks ill as he makes his way over to answer the KNOCKING at the door. When he opens it and sees David and Mary waiting to bring in the Christmas dinner, he brightens.

> DAVID AND MARY
> Merry Christmas!

INT. MCNEIL HOUSE, DAVID'S ROOM - NIGHT

Standing before a canvas on an easel, David is once again plugged into his stereo. As the CAMERA DOLLIES around to look over his shoulder, we see that he is not painting Mary, but rather he has transferred the sketch of his father from the paper to the canvas.

Finishing the sketch, David digs under the bed and comes out with his paint box.

The large, beautifully finished wooden box has seen much service but is well cared for.

Opening the lid, David examines the paint smudged, partially squeezed tubes and the odd assortment of brushes as though they were photographs of old friends. He adds his new brushes to the group.

INT. RIDGE MEMORIAL HIGH, LOCKER ROOM - NIGHT

Away from the others, David is getting dressed in the most remote part of the locker room. Having thrown his gym bag in the lake, he has to make do with a paper shopping bag.

He has trouble with the uniform at first, putting the shirt on backwards. When he gets that squared away, the uniform looks good on him. He's not tall but he has a good build and looks more at home in the uniform than we would have expected, but...

His feet. They're still bare. He reaches for his battered sneakers and colored socks.

He goes to put them on, but before he can do so, a pair of fresh, white, athletic socks land on the bench beside him. David looks up to see Christian.

INT. RIDGE MEMORIAL HIGH GYM, COURT - NIGHT

David is out with the team, warming up in a lay-up drill. On his turn he misjudges the number of strides to the basket, goes too far underneath, and his shot bangs off the underside of the rim.

He trots to the end of the rebound line, directly behind Christian.

>				CHRISTIAN
>		Lighten up.

David looks up at the three-quarter full bleachers.

                    DAVID
          I feel like I'm having one of those dreams
          where you come to school naked. Man,
          Christian, he won't put me in, will he?

                    CHRISTIAN
          If Stephan saw that lay-up you just tried,
          you won't go in unless we got about a
          million point lead.

                    DAVID
          Good.

A LOUD BUZZER SOUNDS. David is startled. The rest of the team drops the basketballs and heads for the bench. David hangs back and begins gathering up the balls.

                    CHRISTIAN
          David!

David runs over and leaves the balls for Dribbles to gather.

The Lancers' cheerleaders fire up the crowd.

                    CHEERLEADERS
          You got the spirit! Let's hear it!

David sits, staring out at the court, for the first time ever noticing how violent the game of basketball can be.

There is a MONTAGE of rough play on the court with the exaggerated violence coming from David's POINT OF VIEW.

A kid gets slammed into the wall pads after completing a lay-up.

Another kid goes up for a rebound and comes down with an elbow in the face. A short guard stands his ground to take an offensive foul from a charging opponent, only to get a knee in the gut.

David cringes in sympathy pain with each injured player. Suddenly the ball flies up and over the Lancer's bench. A Ridge player tries to make a leaping save, but flips over the folding metal chairs of the bench. He crashes on the floor behind David.

As the Ridge player runs off, David looks over to Dribbles, who is seated beside him. Dribbles, with no camera to use, keeps David's old charts.

Dribbles holds up one of the charts and points to David's name. He smiles weakly.

David tries to smile back, but he is not very convincing either.

> DAVID
> Rough game.

Dribbles does not reply. He coughs into a handkerchief.

David looks up to the scoreboard.

CLOSE-UP scoreboard "Home 61, Visitor 66 – Period 4"

> DAVID (CONT'D)
> (sotto voice)
> Thank God it's close.

Dribbles coughs into his handkerchief again. Unseen by anyone else, the handkerchief is spotted with blood.

INT. MCNEIL HOUSE, DAVID'S ROOM - DAY

David is putting the final strokes on the basketball painting of his father. The talent is raw, the technique unrefined, but the passion is immense. Finishing the painting, David steps back to get an overview. He is satisfied.

Something catches his eye. It is Dribbles' smashed camera sitting on the shelf. He picks up the camera and carries it with him over to where he puts his paints away. David looks from the camera to the paint box.

INT. LAKESHORE HIGH GYM, COURT - NIGHT

David and the rest of the team are spread out around the hoop shooting warm-up shots. He is distracted and can't stop looking around.

> DAVID
> Wonder where Dribbles is? Can't believe he'd miss the last regular game.

> CHRISTIAN
> (moves into a jump shot)
> Maybe he just couldn't take the excitement.

Christian's shot swishes.

FLASH FORWARD to the crowd ROARING APPROVAL.

The game is in progress. Michaud steals the ball and takes it all the way down the other end for two.

David applauds Michaud's move. He looks up at the scoreboard.

CLOSE-UP scoreboard "Home 75, Visitor 58 –Period 4"

David looks from the scoreboard to the empty seat where Dribbles should be.

> STEPHAN (O.S.)
> McNeil!

Startled, David looks down to Stephan.

> DAVID
> What?

> STEPHAN
> What d'ya mean, "What?" You're in. For Dwight.

David sits there. A BUZZER SOUNDS.

> STEPHAN (CONT'D)
> Go!

David starts out for the court.

> STEPHAN (CONT'D)
> McNeil!

David turns.

> STEPHAN (CONT'D)
> (motions to the scorer's
> table)
> Check in!

A MONTAGE shows that David comes out onto the court cold and nervous but as he sweats and gets into the game, he loosens up. David guards his man flat-footed. The man blows by him and puts up an open jump shot to score. A Lancer, RUSSO, brings the ball down court. He passes off to David. David tries to pass to Christian, but he is picked off.

Christian brushes by David on the court.

> CHRISTIAN
> Bounce pass next time.

David controls the ball. He dribbles away from one defender, only to be cornered by another. They are sure they have him. Christian waves for the ball. David makes the pass. An opponent tries to steal, but David has bounced the pass and it gets safely to Christian.

The defense swings over to Christian. He throws back over to David who's in the clear. David puts up a shot and scores.

Up in the bleachers, Mary is in the middle of the crowd. When David's shot goes in, her mouth drops open. She smiles and claps.

When David takes off back down the court, he slips and almost falls because of his bald sneakers.

David runs beside Christian on his way down court.

> DAVID
> Not bad, huh?

> CHRISTIAN
> Pick up your man!

David turns to see the man he is supposed to be guarding go in for an uncontested lay-up.

CLOSE-UP scoreboard "Home 79, Visitor 63 – Period 4, 00:15"

Christian puts up a jump shot and scores.

The opposing players hustle bringing the ball down court.

David is guarding his man more closely this time. The boy David is defending makes a bad pass and David steals the ball.

David passes off to Christian.

CLOSE-UP scoreboard "Home - 81, Visitor - 63, Period 4 00:10"

The crowd can be heard CHANTING off the FINAL SECONDS of this last regular game. Christian steams down the court, dribbling. David also runs full throttle. As they approach the basket, the CHANT of the crowd is down to THREE.

Christian passes off to David, who stole the ball, so that he may have the glory. David tries to stop to pop a shot, but his sneakers don't grab.

He slides across the court as though it's ice when the FINAL BUZZER SOUNDS.

The referee is laughing and indicating "traveling".

The crowd cheers for the victory.

Mary is laughing and applauding good-naturedly. She is genuinely impressed with David's guts.

EXT. MCNEIL HOUSE - DAY

Mary trots up to the house carrying a shopping bag from an athletic store. She RINGS THE BELL. David's mother answers the door.

> SARAH
> Hi, Mary. C'mon in.

> MARY
> Hi. Is David home?

> SARAH
>
> He's not. Not yet. But come on in anyway.

Mary enters.

INT. MCNEIL HOUSE, HALLWAY - DAY

Mary digs in the bag and comes out with a shoe-box.

> MARY
>
> Well, my mom's expecting me home, but I was just wondering if you could give him these for me.

She hands the shoe-box to David's mother.

> SARAH
>
> Sneakers?

> MARY
>
> I guessed at the size. The receipt's in there.
> (pause)
> A belated Christmas present – so he can get a better grip on the court.

> SARAH
>
> I'm sorry, I don't understand...

> MARY
>
> You weren't at the game last night?

It's obvious from Sarah's expression that she doesn't understand.

> MARY (CONT'D)
>
> You know, the basketball game?

Sarah is still confused.

> MARY (CONT'D)
>
> You don't know.
> (pause)
> He didn't tell you he made the team?

SARAH
The high school basketball team?

INT. MCNEIL HOUSE, DAVID'S ROOM - DAY

BLACK.

A beam of light pulses across the room. The 8mm movie projector is CHATTERING again. As the CAMERA DOLLIES THROUGH THE GLARE AND AROUND THE BEAM, we see that it is Sarah who is watching the films now.

The light from the projected image reflects in her moist eyes.

She does not cry. She only remembers.

Moving her foot, it brushes against a paper bag. She goes to move the bag out of her way, then pauses. She debates looking inside. Slowly and carefully, she reaches inside the bag and pulls out the top of David's uniform. The image of her husband, as a young man, is washed out on the wall by light leaking in from the silently opening door.

DAVID
I wear the same number, fifty-two.

Sarah is startled.

SARAH
Sorry.
(pause)
Why didn't you tell me?

DAVID
It's no big deal.

SARAH
For a lot of kids it would be. It's not like you, though. I thought you were an artist, not an athlete. How come?

DAVID
I don't know, maybe I felt like I had something to prove.

SARAH
Had?

DAVID
I guess I still do. I'm just not sure I'm
going about it the right way.

Sarah turns the projector off. She opens the window shade to let a little light in on both of them.

DAVID (CONT'D)
Do you think putting a ball through an
iron rim proves anything?

Sarah stops and thinks. She chooses her words carefully.

SARAH
Yes. For some people I think it does.
Setting a goal for yourself, going for it,
and achieving it.

She motions to David's paint box.

SARAH (CONT'D)
But it doesn't have to be basketball. It
could be art.

DAVID
That's why you bought me that?

SARAH
Uh-uh. Just the brushes you got this year.
The paint box was your father's idea.

DAVID
(disbelief)
Dad hated art.

SARAH
He knew you liked it.
(pause)
Different people prove themselves in
different ways.

                        DAVID
            You know what I think? I think
            sometimes it doesn't even have to be a
            thing or an action. Sometimes it can just
            be in the way you treat other people.

Sarah smiles. At this moment, she loves him more than ever.

                        SARAH
            I'd love to come watch you play.

It's David's turn to smile.

EXT. DOWNTOWN LAKESHORE, HOVEY'S PAWN SHOP - DAY

His collar up to guard against the cold wind, carrying his wooden paint box, David walks along the sidewalk and enters the pawn shop.

INT. HOVEY'S PAWN SHOP - DAY

We see, but do not hear, David dicker with the PAWN SHOP OWNER over his paint box. They seem to come to an agreement and then the owner directs David over to the other side of the store. David approaches a glass counter filled with cameras. He examines them briefly and then settles on an VHS movie camera similar to Dribbles' camera which has been destroyed.

EXT. DRIBBLES' APARTMENT - DAY

The Caprice comes to a stop in front of the building. Sarah is driving, David hops out of the passenger side. He's carrying the VHS camera.

David knocks on Dribbles' door but there is no response. He waits a moment and knocks again. Still no response. One more time.

Sarah rolls down the window of the car.

                        SARAH
            You're gonna be late.

                        DAVID
            I guess he already left or something.

David starts to head back to the car when he notices Dribbles' bicycle chained to a hand railing near the door. The bike is covered with snow; it hasn't been moved in days.

David goes back to the door and knocks more frantically this time. No response. He goes to the window and tries to peer in but it's covered with frost. Scared, David breaks in the weak door.

<blockquote>
SARAH
David!
</blockquote>

INT. DRIBBLES' APARTMENT - DAY

David comes rushing into the apartment and sees Dribbles almost immediately. Laying half off the couch, he's either out cold or dead. Surrounding him are his handkerchief and tissues spotted with blood. Some blood is also crusted around the corners of his mouth. Dribbles' hands are lying across his abdomen as if he were pained there.

David comes running over and puts a hand on Dribbles' face. It's still warm. Awkwardly, David checks for a pulse.

He seems to find one. Then, David notices Dribbles' hands. Carefully, he pulls the old man's shirt up over his stomach and sees the bruises. Centers of black, radiating out to purple, then yellow, they are ugly. David recoils. Dribbles, still out of it, coughs.

EXT. LAKESHORE MEMORIAL HOSPITAL - NIGHT

The snow has begun falling again.

INT. LAKESHORE MEMORIAL HOSPITAL, WAITING AREA - NIGHT

People are scattered through the waiting area. Some talk among themselves but in hushed tones. One woman is saying a rosary.

A nurse wheels out a patient who is being released – an older man. A young couple rises to greet him as he enters the waiting area. They are happy but quiet so as not to disturb the others around them who still wait.

David simply sits in a chair and stares out at the snow.

A NURSE walks into the waiting area. She scans the people in the room. David is the only young man.

                    NURSE
               David McNeil?

David's mind had been drifting outside with the snow. He turns and nods.

               NURSE (CONT'D)
          Mr. Stedman would like to see you now.

David rises.

                    DAVID
               Mr. Stedman?

                    NURSE
               Your friend, the man you brought in this
               morning.

A strained smile comes to David as they head for the corridor. The nurse doesn't understand.

                    DAVID
               I guess I forgot his last name. I don't
               even know his first name really.

                    NURSE
               (consults clipboard)
          Herbert.

INT. LAKESHORE HOSPITAL, DRIBBLES' ROOM - NIGHT

David enters the room cautiously. He is intimidated by the intravenous tubes and monitors connected to Dribbles. Dribbles looks old and frail. He is at least cleaned up, though.

Dribbles motions for David to come closer.

                    DRIBBLES
               (with little breath)
          Tuesday.

                    DAVID
          What?

                    DRIBBLES
         Sunday, Monday, Tuesday.
                  (pause)
         Game night.

                    DAVID
         Don't worry about it. How you doin'? I
         thought you were dead.
                  (pause)
         Sorry.

Dribbles BLOWS A RASPBERRY at David. He smiles and then
COUGHS LIGHTLY.

                    DAVID (CONT'D)
         Listen, I wanted to thank you for taking
         over the charts and for the, you know,
         films and everything.

Dribbles' medication is kicking in. He closes his eyes and begins drifting.

                    DRIBBLES
         Thank you, thank you, thank you.

                    DAVID
         For what?

Dribbles merely waves his hand.

INT. LAKESHORE HOSPITAL, CORRIDOR - NIGHT

As David walks past the nurses's station, he notices Principal Becker talking
to a NURSE.

                    PRINCIPAL BECKER
         I'm the principal at Lakeshore High, I was
         told you have a patient – an employee of
         ours.

                    STATION NURSE
         Name?

                    PRINCIPAL BECKER
            Drib...
                    (pause/fumbling for
                    name)
            He's a janitor at the school.

EXT. MCNEIL HOUSE - NIGHT

The Caprice pulls into the driveway and stops. David gets out and walks to the house.

INT. MCNEIL HOUSE, KITCHEN - NIGHT

Sarah is finishing up the dishes. David enters through the side kitchen door.

                    SARAH
            How is he?

                    DAVID
            Not too good. I don't know, at least he
            didn't look good to me.

                    SARAH
            That's too bad.
                    (pause)
            Christian called.

This draws no reaction from David.

                    SARAH (CONT'D)
            You guys won tonight. You're in the
            semi-finals.

She expects something from David, excitement maybe, but gets nothing.

                    SARAH (CONT'D)
            Christian says to tell you, you may get
            your jacket after all.

David smiles absently.

SARAH (CONT'D)
What did he mean?

DAVID
Championship jacket. That's why I joined the team in the first place.

SARAH
Really? Two more games. You may get it. You're playing Friday night aren't you?

DAVID
Yeah, I guess.

Annie enters the kitchen carrying a brown paper shopping bag.

ANNIE
Hey ya kid.

DAVID
Hey Annie.

SARAH
Annie's coming to the game with me too. Aren't you?

ANNIE
We'll see, I may have to work...

SARAH
(surprised)
Annie.

Annie waves for Sarah to hush. David doesn't see this as he heads out of the kitchen.

DAVID
It's O.K., no big deal. Really.

When David is gone.

SARAH
You said...

Annie digs down into the paper bag.

                          ANNIE
                Look what I found at the store.

She opens the bag for Sarah to see.

                       ANNIE (CONT'D)
     Ta-Da!

Looking in the bag, Sarah's jaw drops to her knees.

DISSOLVE TO:

INT. LAKESHORE HOSPITAL, DRIBBLES' ROOM - NIGHT

Dribbles pushes the call button and a LATE SHIFT NURSE we have not seen before enters.

                     LATE SHIFT NURSE
                  How we doin' in here?

Dribbles hands her a scrap of card on which he has written a note.

DISSOLVE TO:

INT. MCNEIL HOUSE, DAVID'S ROOM - NIGHT

David is gathering his uniform together and packing it into his brown paper bag. He pulls the new sneakers Mary has bought for him out of their box, looks at them, and smiles.

                    SARAH (O.S.)
            C'mon. Don't you have to be there early?

                    DAVID
            Coming!

He shoves the sneakers in the bag, grabs a jacket, and heads for the door.

INT. MCNEIL HOUSE, BOTTOM OF STAIRWAY - NIGHT

As David trots down to the bottom of the staircase, Sarah and Annie jump out from around the corner and block his way.

Sarah is wearing jeans, sneakers, and an old, oversized Lancers cheerleader's sweater, complete with a megaphone emblem on the front.

Annie has on a wild assortment of her usual leather and lace combined with a more complete old cheerleader's uniform, including pompoms.

Annie and Sarah cheer wildly.

                    SARAH
            Yea!

                    ANNIE
              (shaking pompoms)
            SIS! BOOM! BAH!

Annie and Sarah calm slightly and model their outfits.

                    SARAH
            Well?

David is speechless.

INT. LAKESHORE HIGH, LOCKER ROOM - NIGHT

The players sit dressed and rounded up, listening to Stephan's pre-game psyche-up. Everyone's heard this speech a million times before on T.V. and in the movies, but every player listens intently. Every player, that is, except for David. David is fascinated by the reactions.

We can see that for him, Stephan's speech is a distant buzzing.

All through the speech, we see CLOSE-UPS of different team members from David's POINT OF VIEW as he studies them.

> STEPHAN
> ...of course you're excited, you'd be crazy not to be. But you get ahead of yourselves and this is the end of the road. Take it one game at a time; don't look beyond tonight.
> (pause/he surveys them)
> Take care of all the small things. Snap those passes, hold out for the high percentage shots, block out, stick every foul shot.

Something Stephan has said catches David's attention and he stops looking to the other players and starts listening to the coach.

> STEPHAN (CONT'D)
> You do all that and you won't have to worry about a championship, you'll already have it.

Stephan's speech goes from a distant buzzing to a clear and powerful volume. David is focused on the coach but he's hearing something that the others aren't.

> STEPHAN (CONT'D)
> A trophy's not important by itself. It's just a symbol of all the basic things you did well along the way – all the small choices you made that were the right choice – how you treated the game.

INT. LAKESHORE HIGH GYM - NIGHT

Sarah sits in the packed bleachers. Annie makes her way recklessly up through the stands, carrying a box of popcorn.

From the crowd's reactions, it is obvious that the game has begun.

An awkward looking teenage boy, sitting with his friends in front of Sarah, gapes at Annie as she climbs around him. Annie smacks the boy with a pompom.

ANNIE
Keep your eyes on the game.

Sarah has her eyes on the court. She is searching, straining to see something.

Her eyes come to rest on what she was looking for and a tense expression comes over her face.

David warms the bench, watching the intensity of his teammates' play. Dribbles' empty seat is beside him once again.

From David's POINT OF VIEW, we see a MONTAGE of the semi-final game.

Christian takes a long jump shot from the outside that arcs high and scores.

The crowd explodes into CHEERS.

An opposing player puts a fake on Michaud, goes up, and scores.

CLOSE-UP scoreboard "Lancers 40, Visitors 42 – Period 2, 00:15"

DWIGHT brings the ball down court for the Lancers. He's hustling, with time running out on the clock. He crosses the half-court line and thinks about a shot but he's guarded too closely.

Dwight passes over to Christian. Christian is immediately double-teamed. He's cornered at the edge of the court. Nowhere to make a pass and nowhere to move, Christian throws the ball at the thigh of one of the men guarding him so it will go out of bounds off of an opponent. Just as the ball heads out of bounds, however, the half-time BUZZER SOUNDS.

CLOSE-UP scoreboard "Lancers 40, Visitors 42 – Period 2, 00:00"

The players head for the locker room and many in the crowd swarm toward the exits.

Mary is battling her way into the gym against the outgoing tide. She's panicked. Her eyes are rimmed red.

Before David makes his way into the locker room, Mary catches up with him. We cannot hear what she says to him over the crowd but whatever it is, he looks worried.

EXT. LAKESHORE HIGH PARKING LOT - NIGHT

David and Mary recklessly jog across the icy lot. David is still wearing his warm-ups, carrying his street clothes in the brown paper bag.

Several fans who hang around outside for a smoke, give the couple strange looks as they head for Mary's car.

EXT. STREETS OF LAKESHORE - NIGHT

Mary's old VW speeds down the slick streets, fishtailing wildly on curves.

INT. MARY'S CAR.

In the front seat, David awkwardly changes from his uniform bottoms into his blue jeans. He wears white cotton briefs under the shorts, rather than a cup.

Whatever is on their minds, it is serious as Mary doesn't even notice that she has a half-naked teenage boy in her car. David hikes up his jeans.

> MARY
> I heard somebody telling Becker it was an emergency; they put him in intensive care.

> DAVID
> Becker on his way there?

> MARY
> Said he couldn't leave the game.

INT. LAKESHORE HOSPITAL, WAITING AREA - NIGHT

David and Mary come rushing into the waiting area. David is still wearing the top to his uniform and warm-up jacket.

They hurry over to a woman who sits behind a reception desk.

> DAVID
> We've come to see Herbert Stedman.

The nurse that first escorted David to the room approaches David and Mary.

>   NURSE
>   David McNeil, right?

David and Mary turn.

>   NURSE (CONT'D)
>   Why don't you take a walk with me,
>   please.

>   DAVID
>   Is he O.K.?

>   NURSE
>   C'mon, there's a conference room just
>   down the corridor.

David and Mary know it's bad and they don't move. They look as though they've just been robbed. The moment hangs.

DISSOLVE TO:

INT. LAKESHORE HIGH GYM - NIGHT

CLOSE-UP scoreboard "Lancers 79, Visitors 86 – a Period 4, 00:00"

The gym is empty save for David and Mary sitting on the painted "L" in the exact center of the court. David is still wearing the warm-up top. They both have been crying a little.

>   DAVID
>   It's kind of weird.

MARY
What?

DAVID
Well, he spent most of his time taking those movies so people would remember the players and who's going to remember him?

MARY
People will...

DAVID
No they won't.
    (pause)
And I don't blame them. Why should they? Who was he anyway? A janitor.

MARY
David!

DAVID
I'm serious. Not mean, just honest. All that stuff in his apartment, the trophies, it's junk. Nobody cares.

MARY
    (crying again)
I care. He was nice to me and I'll remember that.

                    DAVID
          No you won't. In two years you'll be in
          college. You'll be living in an apartment
          with two other girls, wondering if the guy
          in English Literature class is gonna ask
          you out. Wondering how far you'll let
          him go if he does. You'll be thinking
          about if there's gonna be any jobs left by
          the time you graduate, IF you graduate.
                    (pause)
          You'll forget all about high school, let
          alone Dribbles.
                    (pause)
          So will I.

This speech has fired anger in Mary's eyes. But the anger slowly fades and becomes solemnity as she comes to the realization that David is probably right.

Unseen to either of them, Stephan and Christian emerge from the athletic office and walk over toward them.

                    DAVID (CONT'D)
          You're right too, though. He was a nice
          guy and it was good to be around him. It
          made a difference.

                    STEPHAN
          McNeil!

David and Mary turn to see the coach and Christian but neither of them say anything. The coach's voice echoes across the gym.

                    STEPHAN (CONT'D)
          Where were you tonight? Not that it
          mattered.

                    DAVID
          Dribbles is dead. Not that it matters.

The coach and Christian stop and digest this information.

                    STEPHAN
          I'm sorry.

Stephan and Christian continue on over to David and Mary who rise. There is a moment of awkward silence between them as nobody quite knows what to say.

>   CHRISTIAN
>   We lost tonight.

>   DAVID
>   (thinking of more than
>   the game)
>   Yeah, I know.

EXT. LAKESHORE HIGH SCHOOL - DAY

The parking lot is full. Small pockets of students with a free period and an open campus gather here and there to talk and have a smoke.

There is no indication that anyone is even aware of, much less affected by, Dribbles' death.

INT. LAKESHORE HIGH CORRIDOR - DAY

Students TALK, LAUGH, YELL, and SLAM LOCKER DOORS as they swarm from one classroom to another. Large paper banners supporting the Lancers are being ripped down.

At his locker, David is still upset. Not thinking straight, he's having a tough time with his locker door. When he finally manages to get it open, the locker contents spill out onto the floor.

Across the way, Eddie watches David. He then disappears into the crowd.

A BELL RINGS. Students are absorbed into the classrooms.

David is left alone in the corridor, cleaning his books and papers off the floor.

INT. LAKESHORE HIGH, STAIRWELL - DAY

Late for class, David hustles into the stairwell. Not watching where he is going, he runs right into Eddie, who is waiting for him.

> EDDIE
> McNeil. I want to talk to you.

INT. MCNEIL HOUSE, FRONT HALL - DAY

The DOORBELL RINGS. Annie trots down the hall to answer it. She opens the door to find a DELIVERY MAN from the hospital courier service standing there with a package, about the size of a pillow, wrapped in brown paper.

> DELIVERY MAN
> Is a...
>   (checks clipboard)
> David McNeil here?

> ANNIE
> He's at school. I'm his aunt.

> DELIVERY MAN
> I have a delivery from Lakeshore Hospital.

INT. LAKESHORE HIGH, STAIRWELL - DAY

Eddie has walked away from David and is standing under the stairwell. David thinks about making a break for it; he looks around.

He doesn't move though. He's not sure he can run fast enough and there's something about Eddie, in his eyes, that says he's not going to hurt anyone.

David cautiously approaches Eddie under the stairwell.

                    EDDIE
          I heard about the old man. I'm gonna
          turn myself in...

David says nothing. If Eddie's looking for sympathy, he won't get it here.

               EDDIE (CONT'D)
          I don't know what killed him, but I
          imagine it was me.

                    DAVID
          You know that it was.

                    EDDIE
          I'm really scared, man.

                    DAVID
          Oh, that's great. YOU'RE scared.

                    EDDIE
          I used to think it was great. That sort of,
          hold, I had over people. People treated
          me good, you know.
                    (pause)
          But the thing is, half of the them did it
          'cause I could score on the court and half
          of them did it 'cause they were just plain
          scared.

                    DAVID
          I don't understand why anyone would
          want people to be afraid of them.

                    EDDIE
            (explosively/scaring
              David)
        Because it felt good!
            (calms)
        It felt like – power. Then Sheri gets
        pregnant and I fought with her to keep it,
        to save that life...
            (pause)
        ...and what happens? The old guy goes
        and dies.

                    DAVID
        And you're not so much of a hero
        anymore.

                    EDDIE
        No. I guess I never was.

EXT. MCNEIL HOUSE - DAY

Mary's VW pulls over to the side of the road in front of the house.

INT. MCNEIL HOUSE, KITCHEN - DAY

As Mary and David enter and walk past the refrigerator, he stops to read a note stuck there.

                    DAVID
            (reading the note)
        Went to pick up your mother, Annie.
            (pause)
        P.S., There's a package for you in your
        room.

INT. MCNEIL HOUSE, DAVID'S ROOM - DAY

David immediately goes for the pillow-sized package on the bed, but Mary's attention is caught by a drawing sitting on the bookshelf near the door. It is a drawing of her.

                    MARY
        You draw beautifully.

>   DAVID
>   Huh? Oh no, no. You're not suppose...
>
>   MARY
>   Of course I can't say too much for your
>   subject matter.
>
>   DAVID
>   The subject matter is what makes it.

David looks at Mary for a moment, then back to the drawing.

>   DAVID (CONT'D)
>   I feel a lot of passion for this drawing.

They both look to each other. They linger close together. Then Mary moves right on by David and over to the painting of his father.

>   MARY
>   You paint well, too.

David comes over and studies the painting with her.

>   MARY (CONT'D)
>   What do you feel for this one?
>
>   DAVID
>   I don't know about this one. I can never
>   figure out if I love it or if I hate it.
>   (pause)
>   All I know for sure is, I'm glad I did it.

They stand for a moment and Mary kisses his cheek gently.

                    MARY
          Hey, don't forget your package.

She crosses, sits on the edge of the bed, and picks up the package. She reads the return address and a look of concern flows over her face.

                    MARY (CONT'D)
              (holding out the
                package)
          David?

                    DAVID
          What's wrong?

                    MARY
          It's from the hospital.

Sitting down beside her, David carefully tears at the edge of the paper. Pulling back a corner, he finds some aging blue fabric.

                    MARY (CONT'D)
          What is it?

                    DAVID
          I don't believe it.

David rips away some more of the paper and exposes silver embroidery in the blue.

"1985 State Champs - Dribbles Stedman"

He pulls Dribbles' Championship jacket out of the bag.

                    MARY
          Oh my God!

                    DAVID
          What's he giving this to me for?

                    MARY
          Put it on.

A DOOR OPENS and CLOSES downstairs. FOOTSTEPS can be heard on the stairs.

David puts the jacket on. It is sizes too big for him but looks good all the same.

Sarah and Annie appear in the doorway. A small card falls from the paper wrapping that had been around the jacket.

> ANNIE
> Too cool!

> SARAH
> You got your jacket!

> MARY
> Look, a card.

She picks it up. It is Dribbles' card from the hospital.

> SARAH
> Where'd you get that?

> DAVID
> From him. Dribbles.

> SARAH
> How come?

They look at each other in silence. David shrugs. Mary speaks up.

> MARY
> (reading card)
> For being a friend.

INT. DRIBBLES' APARTMENT - DAY

The apartment is SEEN THROUGH THE GRAINY BLACK AND WHITE VIEWFINDER OF A VHS CAMERA. Hand-held and awkward, the camera is obviously in the hands of an amateur as it browses through the apartment.

Close enough on a trophy to read, "Herbert 'Dribbles' Stedman."

Across the autographed backboard and rim.

A bookcase topped with game balls.

The display case filled with uniforms. There is an empty spot where the jacket had once been.

A FADED PHOTOGRAPH OF A SOMEWHAT YOUNGER DRIBBLES IN HIS JACKET AND POSED WITH A BASKETBALL.

The camera holds on this last image for a few moments when suddenly a hand reaches into the frame and grabs the photo.

A CHANGE IN ANGLE no longer uses the VHS view finder and we see that David had been operating the video camera.

While TWO MOVERS carry Dribbles' things out of the apartment, David, wearing the championship jacket, surreptitiously pockets the photo.

EXT. HOVEY'S PAWN SHOP - DAY

Standing in front of the shop, David pops the side door of the camera open and removes the cassette. He closes the camera door and enters the shop.

INT. LAKESHORE HIGH GYM - DAY

We see David's paint box as he reaches into it and pulls out a tube of acrylic paint.

A small glob of white paint is squeezed onto an already heavily used palette of intense colors.

We watch David paint with great concentration. After a while, he stops and steps back to look at his work.

Mary walks up from behind him. She smiles.

                          MARY
                Finished?

David still looks seriously at what he has painted.

                          DAVID
                I think so, yeah.

Mary is obviously pleased with what she sees. David has yet to show emotion.

                          MARY
                I like it. I like it a lot.

David looks from Mary to the painting, then back again. Finally, slowly, he smiles too.

                          DAVID
                It'll do.

David tosses his brush in a jar of water. He and Mary walk off together across the empty gymnasium.

We see David's painting. He has added Dribbles to the mural on the gym's wall. Dribbles' pose comes from the photo David took from the apartment.

Credits roll over a SLOW DOLLY IN to the painting.

FADE OUT.

Production Guide

Filmmaker Biographies

Tom and Heidi Tosi (Producers) are a husband and wife team that has been producing creative projects for almost twenty years. The New Hampshire couple owns and operates Tosi Productions, LLC through which they have produced an award-winning children's web site, educational multimedia games, and short dramatic films which have aired on national television and PBS affiliate stations. Tom holds a degree in filmmaking from Boston University while Heidi has a degree in art from Notre Dame College.

Cast & Crew Biographies

Cast

Joe Orrigo (David McNeil) is a graduate of the American Academy of Dramatic Arts in New York City. He has performed on stage in numerous venues including the Kennedy Center, Boston University, and Smithsonian Discovery Theatre. Making his feature film debut as David McNeil in *Dribbles*, Joe found himself in the demanding position of appearing in virtually every scene of a thirty day shoot.

Eliza Rose Fichter (Mary Todd) won an Elliott Norton award for *Reason* (director Ping Chong), *One Flea Spare* (New Repertory Theater), *The Miracle Worker* (Lyric Stage), and *Russian Tea Party* (Women on Top Theater Festival). She played Biondello in an all-female *Taming of the Shrew* (Boston Theater Works), Marta in Melinda Lopez's *The Order of Things* (winner 1999 Kennedy Center New American Plays), Moth in Mary Zimmerman's *Midsummer Night's Dream* (Huntington Theatre), Emma in *The Curse of the Starving Class* (Chelsea Theater Zone), Antigone in *Oedipus* (American Repertory Theatre), Mary in *Children's Hour* (Lincoln Center, opposite Lynn Redgrave). Filmmaker Darcy Marsh's film of Eliza's performance of *The Russian Tea Party* was a featured event at the Woods Hole Film Festival. Eliza returned to 11th grade at the Cambridge Rindge and Latin High School in January, '07, after being an exchange student in Chile.

Robert Shea (Dribbles) has worked professionally as an actor, director, producer, and performing arts educator for the past 30 years. He currently serves as director of the Dana Center, a regional performing arts center at Saint Anselm College, Manchester, NH. In this capacity, Bob presents some of America's and the world's most accomplished artists in theatre, dance, music, and international folk art. In recent years, Bob served as artistic director for The Barnstormers Theatre in Tamworth, NH, America's oldest professional summer theatre company; and as Vice President for Academic Affairs of the New Hampshire Institute of Art. Bob served as Artistic/ Executive Director of the Palace Theatre, Manchester, NH, from 1983 to 1995. As a young professional, Bob served as director and manager of the New England Repertory Company, a touring American educational theatre company in Great Britain from 1975-1978. In 1980, Bob received a master of fine arts degree from the University of Memphis in performing arts. (www.newarttheatre.com)

Harmony Stempel (Sarah McNeil) graduated from the University of New Hampshire, where she received her Bachelors in Theatre, in May, 2006. Primarily a stage actor, she has performed in *Copenhagen*, *Pterodactyls*, *Stop Kiss*, *The Laramie Project*, *The Tempest*, *Macbeth*, *Rosencrantz & Guildenstern are Dead*, *Tartuffe*, and many other staged productions in New Hampshire and in her home state of New York. Harmony makes her film debut in *Dribbles*. She began exploring film work abroad in the Czech Republic in the spring of 2007. (www.myspace.com/harmleigh)

Victor Warren (Coach Dan Stephan) is a native Californian that has been acting since age ten. He graduated Carnegie Mellon University where he majored in acting and directing. He has appeared in numerous commercials. Some of his TV credits are: *The City*, *Santa Barbara*, *As the World Turns*, *Hunter*, *Backspot Turn*, *General Hospital*, *Unsolved Mysteries* and *The Hill*, which aired for Showtime in 2006. Some of his regional credits include Sam in *Lips Together, Teeth Apart*, Rev. David Lee in *The Foreigner*, Feste in *Twelfth Night*, the Ploughman in *Knives in Hens*. Jess in *The Compleat Works of Willm. Shakspr. (abridged)*. Scrooge in the New England Premiere of *Jacob Marely's Christmas Carol*. Mckenna/Gowen in *Molly Maguire* for the Sugan Theatre Company, Bernie Dodd in *The Country Girl* for the Majestic Theatre, Herbie in *Gypsy*, Jigger Cragin in *Carousel* with Shirley Jones, and Eric Weiss in *Brooklyn Boy* for the Speakeasy stage in Boston. (www.victorwarren.com)

Ben Gettinger (Eddie Coles) graduated from the Theatre and Dance program at the University of New Hampshire in the spring of 2005. During his time at UNH, Ben acted in over a dozen productions. Some of his favorite roles include Claudio in *Much Ado About Nothing*, Tom/Ensemble in *The Rakes Progress*, and Theodore Whitman in *Follies*. When not on the stage or in front of the camera Ben likes to surf, create stand-up comedy routines, read, write, and study art history. *Dribbles* is the first film Ben has had the opportunity to act in. It has been an exciting start to a, hopefully, successful career in the future.

Seth Holbrook (Christian Jones) Born and raised in Melrose, MA, Seth grabbed on to theater and acting at fourteen and has not let go since. Though his personal study of acting is never ending, he was first taught the ropes by his mother (a professional actress and teacher), and later gained more experience during high school. He then continued his studies in both Elmira and Curry College.

Sara Louise Petersen (Annie) graduated with a BA in acting from Emerson College and has gone on to perform in several Boston area productions, including a portrayal of Lika in *The Promise*, by Basement on the Hill Stage, and Lilly in *Lilly's Purple Plastic Purse* by Peterborough Players. She also played Glenna in *Bobby Gould in Hell* and was an ensemble member in *Travesties*, both produced at Williamstown Theatre Festival. She has toured nationally with the Hampstead Players in *Robert Louis Stevenson's Kidnapped*, and most recently played Miss Poppenguhl in Dorset Theatre Festival's production of *Moonlight and Magnolias*.

Steve Gagliastro (Carl Joiner) is thrilled to be making his film debut in *Dribbles*. A versatile actor, vocalist, instrumentalist, composer, and teacher, Gags' experiences include playing Hans/Rudy/Trombone on the Asian National Tour and US Regional Premiere of the Sam Mendes version of *Cabaret*, Wallace Hartley in *Titanic* (Worcester Foothills Theatre), Little Willie in Jack Neary's *Kong's Night Out* (Lyric Stage, Boston), as well as many well received performances around New England with the Steve Gags Jazz Quartet. A resident of Worcester, MA, Steve is a graduate of the University of Massachusetts, Amherst. (sgagliastro@yahoo.com)

Crew

David Hjelm (Director of Photography) has been lighting and shooting professionally for over twenty years. Dave's work has appeared on local, regional, and national television in the U.S. *Dribbles* marks the first time Dave has taken on the role of director of photography for a feature film.

Bruce Simonds (Sound Recording) is working on his first feature film with *Dribbles*. Bruce records music in his home studio in Woodsville, NH. A talented singer/songwriter, Bruce was recognized in 1998 by Nashville's American Songwriter Magazine for his song *It's a Simple Plan*.

Heather Diamond (Production Manager) holds a degree in Business Education from Notre Dame College and teaches both business and computer. Heather's experience made her well suited to the role of production manager. *Dribbles* is Heather's first feature film.

Ben Hjelm (Assistant Director) has directed numerous short films at a young age. Ben attended the Performance PLUS summer training program in film at the New Hampton school, working with guest artist Ernest Thompson, writer of *On Golden Pond*. When not working on films, Ben can often be found creating other forms of visual art or playing music on trumpet and French horn.

Jennifer St. Cyr (Hair & Makeup) handled hair and make-up chores for her first feature film with *Dribbles*. Jen is privy to (and guards closely) many secrets of the cast and looks forward to seeing them again and doing more work for screen.

Music

John Sharpley (Original Score)
Originally from Houston, Texas, USA, Sharpley has resided in Singapore since 1986. His personal collection of over 250 musical instruments, mostly from Southeast Asia, reflects his research and passion for Asian music.

He is currently a visiting music lecturer at the Nanyang Academy of Fine Arts. He was Assistant Professor of Music at Boston University and Composer-in-Residence at LaSalle College of the Arts (Singapore). As a solo pianist, he tours regularly, performing his own works to much acclaim.

Sharpley's compositions include orchestral works, opera, music for theatre, film and dance scores, chamber music, songs, and solo piano works. The Houston Symphony Orchestra, the St.Petersburg Philharmonic (Russia), the Sheffield Winds (Chicago), the Singapore Symphony Orchestra, and the China Philharmonic Orchestra are some of the prominent ensembles which have performed Sharpley's compositions. This prolific and versatile musician collaborates with artists from a wide variety of art forms and genre. He has worked extensively with dancers/choreographers, Maxine Heppner and Lim Fei Shen. (www.johnsharpley.com)

The Whatnot (Featured Songs)
The acoustic trio, based out of Portsmouth, NH, successfully blends acoustic and electric instruments to create a sound that is much larger than the sum of its parts. The genre is fun upbeat pop music and the group is extremely versatile, as demonstrated in their performance settings ranging from intimate coffee houses and bar gigs to 1500 seat theaters and college gymnasiums. The Whatnot is: **Chris Mathews** on percussion, **Matt Junkin** on bass, and **Patrick Curry** on guitar, with all three members lending their vocal talents to original songs. The band formed in November of 2002. (www.thewhatnot.com)

The Everyday Visuals (Featured Songs)
The Everyday Visuals is a group of five young gentlemen playing rock music with independent spirit. The current line up was formed in the spring of 2006:

Christopher Pappas (Vocals, guitar, keyboards) has an irrational fear of being a passenger in a fast moving car and cries every time he hears the *Durfle Requiem*.

Eli Scheer (Guitar, vocals, keyboards) has a family member in every U.S. time zone and likes to meet people with a good story to tell.

Joseph Seiders (Drums, vocals, keyboards) should eat more vegetables and panics when he feels his heart beating.

Chris Zembower (Bass, vocals) would rather read a textbook than a fiction novel and doesn't run when he gets caught in the rain.

Kyle Fredrickson (Guitar, keyboards) is frequently late and at age 16 hid the first electric guitar he bought from his mother for three months. (www.theeverydayvisuals.com)

Production Notes

In the summer of 2004, Tom and Heidi Tosi began pre-production on the feature-length drama, *Dribbles*. This husband and wife team from New Hampshire has combined rich backgrounds in art, storytelling, and technology to create award-winning interactive web sites for children and short films that have aired nationally in the U.S., on PBS affiliate stations, and won laurels in both domestic and international film festivals. While the couple has a strong history of looking primarily to themselves when producing creative projects, tackling a live-action, feature-length drama would require considerable assistance.

Cast

Casting would be the first challenge. From small, informal sessions at local high schools, colleges, and universities, to attending much larger sessions in Boston, the couple viewed the auditions of over five hundred actors from around New England and New York to fill the nine featured roles.

Working with a special agreement from the Screen Actors Guild, designed specifically to encourage small-budget independent production, the *Dribbles* cast was able to combine both union and non-union talent.

Joe Orrigo, a recent graduate of the American Academy of Dramatic Arts in New York City, was cast in the lead role playing the character of David McNeil. "We held the call-back auditions in the gymnasium of a small elementary school," Tom said. "What's funny," he recalled, " is that Joe was called back to read for the part of David and David's pretty much the one guy that's not supposed to be able to play basketball. So, here we are in this small school gym for a casting session and Joe finds a loose ball while waiting for his turn. He starts to shoot and it's immediately obvious that he's probably the best player there. We had a shortage of good actors who could actually play basketball, so we had Joe read for several roles. He blew us away and could have taken one of several parts but, after reviewing the footage from that day, we knew he was our David."

Playing opposite Joe, in the role of self-confident, new-girl-at-school, Mary, is Eliza Rose Fichter. "What's great about Eliza for this particular role," Heidi pointed out, "is that she is an incredibly talented and experienced actress who is still actually a high school student. By the time we saw her, Eliza had already won a number of prestigious awards for her work and had a long list of credits that included performing at the American Repertory Theater and at the Lincoln Center in New York City with Lynn Redgrave." Tom remembers Eliza walking through the door at the first cast read-through of the script. "Several other cast members, who had not yet seen Eliza, met her and just knew immediately, without being told, that she would be playing Mary. That's when I knew we cast well, when actors didn't have to ask each other what part they were playing."

Crew

The key crew positions on *Dribbles* were much easier to fill. For the director of photography, Tom and Heidi turned to David Hjelm, a long-time friend with over twenty years experience lighting and shooting for local, regional, and national television. On sound, they tapped Bruce Simonds, who the couple knew to be an award-winning songwriter familiar with recording music in his home-based studio. "We approached Dave and Bruce," Tom explained, "not only because they would deliver the images and sound needed but also because we knew these guys are the kind of people you need on the set – rock solid work ethic with a sense of humor. There's just no underestimating the value of that stabilizing force in the chaos of production."

Locations

Shooting a feature film entirely on location is always an intimidating prospect and this is especially so when that location is New England during the fall and winter. One of the great success stories of *Dribbles*, however, is the naturalism imbued in the film from the environment in which it was shot.

Dribbles was shot from October to December in 2005 all around the state of New Hampshire in real high schools, colleges, homes, streets, and playgrounds.

Filming in functioning high schools could not, of course, take place during school hours so the film crew worked many days from 3pm to 11pm to recreate crowded hallways, bake sales, basketball tryouts, games, and cheering crowds.

Universities allowed the crew to shoot car scenes on little-used private campus roads enabling the production to avoid the difficulties associated with closing public roadways for filming.

Private homes opened their doors to the film. In the case of the McNeil house, a home in Portsmouth, NH served as the exterior, downstairs and attic, while a home three hours away in Woodsville, NH, portrayed David's room in the same "movie" house.

Location shooting for *Dribbles* could not possibly have happened without generous cooperation from the State of NH Film Office, the U.S. Army

Corps of Engineers, various cities and towns, colleges and universities, high schools, middle schools, elementary schools, and many private individuals in the state.

Music

The music of *Dribbles* needed to reflect the same naturalism as the rest of the production. Live music played during the shoot by pep bands was written by New Hampshire composer David Heintz. For the rock songs, the Tosi's again turned to area musicians. New England based groups The Whatnot and The Everyday Visuals provide a total of seven tunes for the soundtrack.

The instrumental score would not be local. For that, Tom and Heidi contacted an old friend literally halfway around the world. Singapore composer John Sharpley was charged with writing the emotional score for the film. "John and I first collaborated on *The October Garden* – a short student film made while we were both at Boston University," Tom said. "John is an extremely well-educated and experienced composer. What's even more valuable, though, is his innovation and enthusiasm." The Houston Symphony Orchestra, the St. Petersburg Philharmonic (Russia), the Sheffield Winds (Chicago), the Singapore Symphony Orchestra, and the China Philharmonic Orchestra are some of the prominent ensembles which have performed Sharpley's compositions. He has also worked with the rock group R.E.M., composing an arrangement for the song *Lotus*.

Motion Picture End Credits

Dribbles Credits[1]

produced by
Heidi & Thomas Tosi

cast

David McNeil	Joe Orrigo
Mary Todd	Eliza Rose Fichter
Dribbles	Robert Shea
Sarah McNeil	Harmony Stempel
Coach Dan Stephan	Victor Warren
Eddie Coles	Ben Gettinger
Christian Jones	Seth Holbrook
Annie	Sara Louise Petersen
Carl Joiner	Steve Gagliastro
Skater Kid	Sean Callahan
Sherri	Katie Martin
Michaud	Zack McQueary
Civics Girl	Kelly Richards
Dwight	Scott Hambleton
Principal Becker	Pat Tierney
Bus Driver	Frank S. Aronson
Store Manager	Richard Arum
Check Out Girl	Ariel Harrist
Locker Girl #1	Jeannie Marie Clark
Locker Girl #2	Lily Kathryn Noble
Head Cheerleader	Ashley VandeBogart
Nurse #1	Stephanie Gould
Nurse #2	Jennifer Matzke
Alex McNeil	Andy McLeavey
Kid in Crowd	Matt Musty
Harve	Gary M. Bouchard
Sink Kid	Jay Bouchard
Kid on Bike	Kevin Turner
Bake Sale Lady	Mary Turner

written & directed by
Thomas Tosi

---

[1] credits as of December 14, 2006

art direction by
Heidi Tosi

director of photography
David Hjelm

music by
John Sharpley

sound recording by
Bruce Simonds

production manager
Heather Diamond

edited by
Thomas, Heidi, & Lincoln Tosi

assistant director
Ben Hjelm

hair & makeup by
Jennifer St. Cyr

background performers

Naiara Campo Albala	Kathy Locke
Kasi Allison	Shannon Locke
Cal Anderson	Kerianne Mack
Melissa Anderson	Melanie Magoziarz
Eric Bartolotti	Nathan Mann
Matthew Bartolotti	Philip Matzke
Vincent Bartolotti	Heather Mazersky
Jeffrey Beasley	Robert McCardell
Diane G. Beaudin	Bonnie McLellan
Amiee Belanger	Jonathan A. McNerney
Jason Beliveau	Kelley Mitchell
Zac Bennett	Chelsea Murfitt
Erin Berger	Matt Musty
Kirsten Bielarski	Rochelle Neveu
Erika E. Boisvert	Taylor Parnell
Aaron Bonta	Amanda Payea
Angelina Bossone	J. Paul Pelletier
Joshua Bouchard	Courtney Perron

Philip Bouchard
Julia Bowman
Kaylin Bull
Lindsay Burns
John A. Callanan, Jr.
Samantha Catterall
Mariah Brennan Clegg
Christopher Colby
Erin Coutu
Thaddeus J. Curry
Thomas D'Angelo
Joseph D'Angelo
Carina Demarais
Heather Diamond
Paul Diamond
Mary-Beth Dickey
Jacki Douglas
Benjamin Elliot IV
Amanda Fisher
William Gilbert
Alyssa Gleason
Amanda Grady
Leandra Mona Haupt
David Heintz
Michael Heintz
Jorine Hilhorst
Ben Hjelm
David Hjelm
Sarah Hjelm
Taylor Horne
Kendra Hotchkiss
Dimitrios Kapotis
Ari Kinder
Corrie Kinder
Jan Kinder
Jim Kinder
Miranda Kinder
Pam Kinder
Kathleen Kolman
Adrien Kordas
Edith Moore Kuzma
Carol LeBarron
Jennifer Lynn Leclerc

Cindy Cartier Petersen
Christopher M. Pike
Emily Pion
Joey Plunkett
Tom Quigley
Bailey Quinn
Nancy B. Ranno
Ray
James F. Rheaume
Terry Rheaume
Patrick Riggie
Donald Robinson
Mary Anne Robinson
Rosie
N. Keegan Routhier-O'Connell
Ashley Scruton
Chelsi Shedd
Bruce E. Simonds
Bruce H. Simonds
Cindy Simonds
Hilda Simonds
Lisa Simonds
Molly Simonds
Nelson R. Simonds
Ian Smith
Sam Smith
Jennifer St. Cyr
Amanda Stuart
Rachel Thompson
Heidi Tosi
Lincoln Tosi
Meaghan Tosi
Thomas Tosi
Shaun Trapletti
Alex Valliant
Chrissy Valliant
Stacy Vargus
Michelle Vesterdal
Irene Vitale
Kate W.
Ryan Washer
Justin Woods
Amanda Wurtz

Selina Lemay
Jen Lloyd
David Locke, Jr

Haley Wurtz
Kayla Wurtz
Sandy Z.

casting by
Thomas & Heidi Tosi

casting assistance
Robert Shea/Saint Anselm College
Jennifer Matzke/John Stark Regional High School
David Kaye/The University of New Hampshire
Robert Lawson/Franklin Pierce College
Stage Source - Boston
Lisa Simonds

scenic artists
Heidi Tosi
Sue Hjelm
Sarah Hjelm
Ben Hjelm
Meaghan Tosi

wardrobe
Heidi Tosi
Bruce Simonds
Heather Diamond

food services
Bruce Simonds
Heidi Tosi
Heather Diamond
Lisa Simonds
Linda C. Hicks/Southern New Hampshire University

production interns
Anne Shea
Jennifer LaBranche
Matthew D. Naughton

location assistance
John Stark Regional High School
Southern New Hampshire University
U.S. Army Corps of Engineers
City of Portsmouth, NH
Haverhill, NH Coop Middle School
State of New Hampshire Film Office
Lanctots Market
Hall's Radio & Television Service
Kathleen & Jerold Tostenson
Bruce & Lisa Simonds
Bruce & Hilda Simonds
Arthur Aaronson
Amy Hannon
Ed VanSickler
Brian Spain
J Paul Pelletier
Bill Raycraft
Al Lanctot
Steve Caggiano

songs
"Peaceful"
written by Patrick Curry
performed by The Whatnot
cello arrangements by Dan Prindle appearing courtesy of Tides Records
copyright 2003 Huesen Records

"Feeling Fine"
written & performed by The Whatnot
copyright 2003 Huesen Records

"So Fast"
written & performed by The Whatnot
copyright 2003 Huesen Records

"Headstrong And Heartweak"
words & music by Christopher Pappas
performed by The Everyday Visuals
copyright 2006 Night Racer Music

"(I Hide My) Smile"
words & music by Christopher Pappas
performed by The Everyday Visuals
copyright 2004 Night Racer Music

"Electric Lights"
words & music by Christopher Pappas
performed by The Everyday Visuals
copyright 2004 Night Racer Music

"Beautiful Day #1"
words & music by Christopher Pappas
performed by The Everyday Visuals
copyright 2004 Night Racer Music

"One Shot"
music by David Heintz
performed by the Woodsville High School Pep Band
copyright 2005 David Heintz

david mcneil artwork by
Heidi Tosi

payroll services
American Residual & Talent, Inc

special thanks
John Stark Regional High School
Southern New Hampshire University
The University of New Hampshire
Saint Anselm College
New Hampshire Community Technical College
Villa Augustina School
Stage Source - Boston
The State of New Hampshire Film Office
The Town of Woodsville, NH
The City of Portsmouth, NH
Goffstown Truck Company

Goffstown Village Cuts
DF Custom Embroidery
Apothēca Flower Shoppe & Tea Chest
Hill-Brook Motel
Nootka Lodge

special thanks to
Dr. Paul J. LeBlanc
Dr. Scott J. Kalicki
Dr. Ausra Kubilius
Justine Wood-Massoud
Harry Umen
Arthur Aaronson
Amy Hannon
Ed VanSickler
Brian Spain
J Paul Pelletier
Bill Raycraft
Gregg Mazzola
Norman H. St. Onge, Jr.
Dr. Landis Magnuson
Dr. Gary M. Bouchard
Lisa Simonds
Matthew Newton
Jan Phelps
Joan Debow
Alister Shanks
Brad Clark
Thomas Hall
John P. Bohenko
Bruce E. Simonds
Hilda Simonds
Jack Daniels
Sr. Pauline Ayotte, RJM
Jim Gallagher
Bruce C. Labs
Carolyn Babcock
Tom St. Cyr

Special Thanks to the Screen Actors Guild

DRIBBLES
a
Tosi Productions, LLC
presentation

The events depicted in this movie are fictitious. Any similarity to any person living or dead is merely coincidental.
screenplay copyright 2003 Thomas Tosi
motion picture copyright 2007 Heidi Tosi & Thomas Tosi

www.ingramcontent.com/pod-product-compliance
Lightning Source LLC
Chambersburg PA
CBHW030939090426
42737CB00007B/477